The Politics of Nonpartisanship

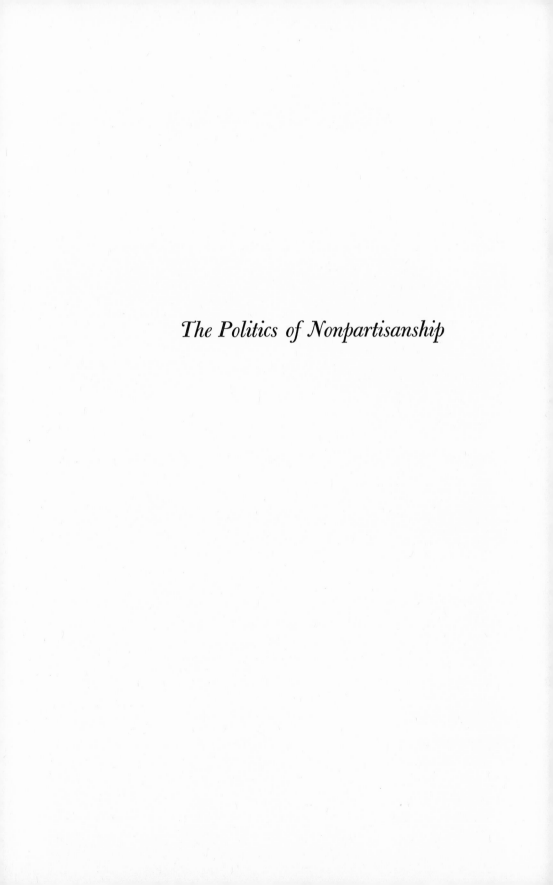

Eugene C. Lee

THE POLITICS OF NONPARTISANSHIP

A Study of California City Elections

University of California Press
Berkeley and Los Angeles

1960

University of California Press
Berkeley and Los Angeles, California
Cambridge University Press • London, England

©1960 BY THE REGENTS OF THE UNIVERSITY OF CALIFORNIA

Library of Congress Catalog Card Number: 60-14380
Printed in the United States of America
Designed by Marion Jackson Skinner

To Jane

Acknowledgments

This book was published with the aid of a publication grant from The John Randolph Haynes and Dora Haynes Foundation. The author wishes to express his gratitude to the Board of Trustees and, particularly, to the Committee on Research and Grants of this foundation. Grateful acknowledgment is also given for the support received from the special fund made available by the Rockefeller Foundation to the Department of Political Science of the University of California at Berkeley, which enabled the author to devote the time necessary for the final preparation of the manuscript.

Advising on the original formulation of the project, the conduct of the investigation, and the presentation of the findings were, at various stages, Professors George Belknap, Herbert Blumer, Victor Jones, Joseph P. Harris, Warren Miller, and John Vieg. The field work was made possible through the coöperation of several hundred civic leaders throughout California—mayors, city managers, newspaper editors, political party chairmen, and many others. Special thanks are due to those persons in the cities of Berkeley, Chico, Fresno, Maywood, Pomona, and San Leandro who contributed so generously of their time and knowledge to provide for the author a picture of local politics in their communities. Friendly help was received throughout the study from Richard Carpenter and Howard Gardner of the League of California Cities. Roger Kent and Thomas Caldecott, state chairmen of the two political parties at the time of the field work, were equally coöperative.

One does not fully appreciate until one has been through the mill the importance of technical assistance in the preparation of a publication. Maxwell E. Knight of the University of California Press, Editorial Department, was a patient and persevering editor against, it is hoped, not insuperable odds. Lloyd Lyman, Assistant to the Director of the Press, provided timely and wise guidance on numerous occasions. Special appreciation must be extended to typists Dorothy Pollard and Nancy McCullough who led the manuscript through several revisions, while maintaining their sense of humor. To the Bureau of Public Administration's research and library staff, generally, and its director Dwight Waldo, thanks are given for the encouragement and support afforded this project.

Berkeley, California   E. C. L.

Contents

Appendixes

Tables

THE SETTING

1

Introduction

THIS IS THE AGE OF THE URBAN COMMUNITY. THE CITY is home for one hundred and ten million Americans. Most of the remaining seventy million measure their lives by urban standards. While only two-fifths of the nation's population lived in cities at the turn of the century, nearly two-thirds do in 1960. The number of incorporated towns and cities has more than doubled in the past fifty years, and the tide of urbanization flows even faster.

Municipal complications multiply with an exploding population, and the prospect is for an increase of another twenty-five million in the decade of the 'sixties. What to do? Even to list a few of the more urgent urban problems—planning and zoning, traffic and mass transit, air and water pollution, slum clearance and redevelopment, juvenile delinquency and race relations—must make the average city dweller feel that he is on a treadmill and will have to run hard to stay even. The solution or amelioration of these problems will necessitate action at all levels of government as well as in the sphere of private effort. None will be resolved unless local units are prepared to play their full role. Despite the increasing dominance of federal programs and policies, the nation's cities will continue to be of enormous importance in shaping the character of American culture.

Even without the extraordinary pressures of the present day, however, the normal and continuing services of urban government—education, law enforcement, public works, public health, parks, recreation, and libraries—contribute impressively toward determining the quality of national life.

Both the resolution of current issues and the conduct of normal municipal activities will be governed by politics. Who shall make the controlling decisions? What kind of decisions shall be made? How shall they be implemented? These questions are the essence of the political process. They are worthy of careful inquiry and analysis.

Yet, we know surprisingly little about them. Writing in 1948, for example, V. O. Key observed that "about all that can be concluded about voting in state and local elections is that scholars have a wonderful opportunity to narrow our area of ignorance." [1] And a decade later, another student of local poltitics reported the same situation. "Unquestionably," says Robert Wood in his book *Suburbia,* "the most significant point to be made is how little systematic and reliable knowledge we have about suburban politics. . . . Except for bits and pieces of information, the field is open for the exercise of logic and speculation." [2]

At the heart of the urban political process, of course, is the city election. Candidate selection, campaigning, and voting cannot be said to comprise the sum and substance of local politics. Yet the choice as to who should hold public office is, generally speaking, the most important political decision the community makes. Fortunately for the student of politics, it is also an event which can

---

[1] Key, *Politics, Parties and Pressure Groups* (1948), p. 614.
[2] Wood, *Suburbia: Its People and Their Politics* (1958), pp. 195, 176.

be systematically described and investigated, because the election and the events leading to it constitute indentifiable and isolable phenomena in the stream of political behavior.

Study of local elections is prompted, however, by yet another reason, namely the existence in more than 60 per cent of the nation's cities of a ballot, separate and distinct from that employed in almost all state and national elections—the nonpartisan ballot. Strictly speaking, a nonpartisan election is one in which no party label appears on the ballot, and candidates are normally nominated by a simple petition process. In theory, however, and to some extent in practice, the nonpartisan election is more. It amounts to a system, indeed a political philosophy, aiming to establish and strengthen direct voter-candidate ties, free from the intervening influence of any organized group, particularly of national political parties.

If there is "little systematic and reliable knowledge" about local politics generally, information concerning nonpartisan elections is almost nonexistent. One of the most diligent observers of the current scene declares that no attempt has been made to integrate this particular phenomenon into the total pattern of American politics and that almost no material is available upon which to make generalizations.[3] Suggestive of this is the failure—whether as a result of intent or oversight—of the American Political Science Association report, *Toward a More Responsible Two-Party System,* to give any attention to community politics or even to mention nonpartisan elections.[4]

At the moment, consequently, the student trying to evaluate the idea of the nonpartisan election has little more to go on than did Beard and Merriam when they took their opposing stands on the question a quarter-century ago. "I am prepared to defend the thesis," wrote Charles A. Beard in 1917, "that nonpartisanship has not worked, does not work, and will not work in any major city in the United States." But Charles E. Merriam, drawing on his experience in Chicago politics, argued: "The lines that divide men in national affairs do not run in the same direction [in municipal

---

[3] Adrian, "A Typology for Nonpartisan Elections," *Western Political Quarterly,* XII (June, 1959), 449.

[4] American Political Science Association, *Toward a More Responsible Two-Party System* (1950).

affairs], and the attempt to force them to do so has been a conspicuous failure in this country." [5]

One point remains clear, however. "The political process goes on here [in the city] as it does at all levels. . . . Different groups in the community want different things. Therefore, each encourages persons that it approves of to run for office and helps them in their campaigns." [6] Whatever the motives of the early founders of the nonpartisan movement, politics continue to be the basis of the whole local election process, regardless of the type of ballot used.

This book presents the results of a study of nonpartisan politics in the cities of one state—California. It first attempts to describe the local election process, answering such questions as these: What kinds of groups and persons engage in local politics and what do they do? What types of campaigning characterize local elections? What similarities and contrasts are apparent between partisan politics, state or national, and nonpartisan municipal politics? What are the special characteristics of voting behavior in local elections? On the basis of this description, local elections are then evaluated against several accepted norms of democratic practice, such as the genuineness of political competition and the potential access to power of all groups in the community. Finally, an effort is made to compare nonpartisan elections in practice with the basic theory of nonpartisan politics.

In addition to shedding a beam of light on the local election process, the book hopefully illuminates, however faintly, relationships between city politics and state and national politics. It is clear that this relationship exists despite the nonpartisan character of local elections. The voter's mind is not divided into water-tight compartments as he considers issues and casts his ballot for candidates for local, state, or national office. Nor are the political leaders of a city or its various groups and associations so divided. Differentiations are plentiful and significant, but the political process does not respect governmental levels. It is inherently indivisible. If this be accepted, a study of community politics will

---

[5] Beard, "Politics and City Government," *National Municipal Review,* VI (March, 1917), 205; Merriam, *A More Intimate View of Urban Politics* (1929), p. 99.

[6] Walker and Cave, *How California is Governed* (1953), p. 226.

yield increased insights in the broader political processes of both state and nation.

By way of introduction, it is essential to describe the climate in which California city politics take place, to portray the background of the nonpartisan movement, and to sketch the methods and procedures utilized in the study.

2

California 1960

KNOWLEDGE OF THE ENVIRONMENT, ALWAYS IMPORTANT
to an understanding of local politics, is a compelling necessity in
California. Such has been the impact of rapid change that analysis
and generalization can be valid only if the total political context
is kept in mind. The attempt at description is often dated by the
time the task is completed. The frequently fragmentary and in-
conclusive character of the data illustrates the dramatic shifting
of the scene. The following pages highlight some of the important
features of the California setting in which "the politics of nonpartisanship" take place.

THE STATE SCENE

Area and Population.—California is third in size among the fifty states, and has an area of more than 150,000 square miles. It is larger than Illinois, Iowa, and Ohio combined. New England would fit within its borders, and one of its fifty-eight counties alone would encompass Connecticut, Massachusetts, and New Jersey. Corresponding to the size of the state is its diversity of topography, climate, and resources.

More important than size or diversity is population growth.[1] Since the historic boom of the Gold Rush, which saw the number of non-Indians increase from 15,000 to 250,000 between 1849 and 1852, it has been this growth and particularly the impact of migration from other states which has most strikingly shaped the history of the state and its institutions. While the United States increased two and one-half times in population from 1900 to 1960, California's population increased more than ten times. In 1950, the census reported a figure of ten and one-half million, in 1960 of more than fifteen and one-half million—a growth averaging a half million each year. The phenomenon continues to be the most important single influence on the life of the state, as suggested by the prediction that by 1970 California will number twenty-two million and will be the most populous state in the nation. Most of this growth will result from in-migration. In 1950, only three-eighths of the population were native to the state, and in 1960 in-migration continued to account for 60 per cent of the population increase.

From the outset, California has been more highly urbanized than the nation, even in 1860, the date of the first complete state census. Today, more than 80 per cent of the state's population live in urban areas; California is one of the five most urbanized states. Also, during most of its history the state has had a far larger proportion of its population in metropolitan areas than has been true for the United States as a whole. During the 1950's, 90 per cent of the state's growth occurred in these population centers. Within the metropolitan areas, in California as across the nation,

---

[1] Most population data cited below are based on information in Thompson, *Growth and Changes in California's Population* (1955).

most of this recent growth took place outside the central cities. For example, in the nine-county Bay Area, the cities of Oakland and San Francisco actually lost population in the decade of the 1950's, while population in the remaining portions of the Bay Area rose by more than 60 per cent. In Los Angeles County, the city of Los Angeles gained by one-quarter, other parts of the county by two-thirds.

These population shifts are caused not only by the pattern of initial settlement of migrants but also by the Californians' tendency to move from one area to another within the state (often from central city to suburbs)—a tendency much greater in California than in other states.

As with cities throughout the nation, internal changes have featured California's urban growth. In contrast to a white population increase of 50 per cent from 1940 to 1950 and 40 per cent from 1950 to 1960, the comparable gains in Negro population were 275 per cent in the decade of the 'forties and 75 per cent in the 'fifties. From 1.8 per cent of the total population in 1940, the Negro percentage increased to 4.4 in 1950 and to more than 5 in 1960. More than 90 per cent of the Negroes in the state are concentrated in the metropolitan areas. In the 'fifties, increases in Negro population in many California cities were from two to five times those of the white population. It is in these places, of course, that the impact of racial change on the political life of the community has been most profound.

Economy.—The rate of California's population growth has always been related to the national economy and the state's position in it, and the mentioned increases during the past decade have been paralleled by developments in the commercial and industrial life of the state. Reflecting the high degree of urbanization and the relatively high per-capita income, employment in distributive and service occupations was relatively higher (60 per cent) than in the nation (50 per cent), while the state consistently ranked in the top five or six in manufacturing. The aircraft and electronics industries have been heavily represented; in 1957, 23 per cent of all national employment in these branches was California-based. Even so, California still retains its position as the leading farm state of the country in terms of cash farm income, and food processing constitutes one of the major areas of manufacturing.

Government and Politics.—Population growth and an expanding economy bring not only opportunities, but a full measure of problems: traffic, smog, water, schools, land use, and many more. At the same time, the growth shapes the political institutions, the state and local governments, which must assume the leadership in meeting these same problems.

At the state level, California's governmental structure resembles the pattern found throughout the United States. A bicameral legislature with an upper house based almost entirely on area representation, a divided administration resulting from the direct election of six key officers, and a large number of independent boards and commissions—these are all familiar to students of state government. Exceptional, perhaps, is the degree to which the state's civil-service system has been extended and its general high quality; the growing tendency of legislative posts to become almost full-time, particularly because of the frequent use of interim committees; the degree of professionalization of certain legislative staff offices; the widespread use of the initiative, referendum, and amending process and a corresponding state constitution both lengthy and detailed.

A review of the state's political institutions reveals a more individual picture. Writing in 1955, Harris noted in his *California Politics* the existence of cross-filing—an election system in which state and Congressional candidates regularly ran in the primaries of both major parties and often captured both nominations, virtually eliminating a contest long before the November general election. Harris also made the following points: A substantial majority of voters (59 per cent of the two-party total in 1958) were registered Democrats, yet Republicans had been highly successful in controlling the state government for many years; because of a relatively new and unstable population and because of organizational factors, the political parties were relatively weak; as a result, politics had become highly personalized with a heavy reliance not on the political party but on mass media and professional public-relations organizations; in both parties extralegal organizations had arisen which had "largely superseded" the official party machinery; and the almost exclusively Republican press and numerous pressure groups assumed a relatively larger role in California than elsewhere.[2]

---

[2] Harris, *California Politics* (1955).

Less than five years later, however, the revised edition of *California Politics* reports "the end of an era in California politics." [3] The decade of the 'fifties had witnessed an abrupt and intense shift in political patterns and processes with little parallel in the history of the nation's states.

Cross-filing, perhaps the most distinctive feature of California's past political landscape, was abolished by the 1959 legislature. The attempt of candidates of one party to capture the nomination of the other party, thereby avoiding the necessity to campaign in the general election, had already largely been nullified by an initiative measure that placed on the 1954 and later primary ballots, hitherto "nonpartisan" in a sense, the party affiliation of the candidates for state and national office. The impact of this seemingly minor change was as dramatic as it was abrupt, although a direct cause-effect explanation would be an oversimplification. Whereas in 1952 almost 75 per cent of state and national legislative races had been concluded in the primary, the figures were reversed in 1954 with party labeling required, and 73 per cent of the legislative races were forced into the general election. The trend continued, and in 1958 only 22 per cent of the races were decided by successful cross-filing (or lack of a contest).

The decade of the 'fifties saw a resurgence of Democratic strength in the legislature, the Congressional delegation and, finally, the state-wide administrative offices. The proportion of legislative offices held by the Democrats, only 32 per cent in 1952, reached a peak of 60 per cent in the 1958 sweep. Only one Republican, the incumbent secretary of state, held a state-wide office (there are six partisan offices) following the November elections, and Democrats were in complete control of the state government for the first time in recent history. In 1958, at least, the phenomenon of registered Democrats consistently voting Republican was upset. In fact, primary election results and later public-opinon polls indicated more Republicans voting for the Democratic gubernatorial candidate than vice versa.

The Democratic upsurge in the 'fifties was marked by a strengthening of party organization and leadership. This included the development of the unofficial and extralegal club movement, organized into the California Democratic Council and including

---

[3] Harris and Rowe, *California Politics*, 2d ed., rev. (1959), p. 1.

within its ranks 40,000 members. By 1960, the Republican party, badly rent by intraparty strife in 1958, had regrouped forces and gave every evidence of returning to its former effectiveness.

Two-party competition in California seems assured, and the historical characterization of the state's allegedly "weak" parties requires substantial amendment. Republicans and Democrats also have moved closer to the traditional role of political parties than a short decade ago. Party caucuses and increased party-line voting have featured recent sessions of the legislature. Leaders in both camps are stressing the need for stronger party organization, and a possible reorganization of the currently fragmented and formless structure of the county and state committees is being studied. Campaign organizations built around a candidate and his personal entourage will continue to dominate many races, yet the party slate and party-oriented and -financed campaigns will unquestionably be more emphasized in the future.

Partisan attitudes and behavior are accelerated by two other factors. California has become the home of leading presidential candidates, is gaining an ever-larger voice in the national conventions, and is now a favored site for the conventions themselves.

Secondly, California's Congressional delegation is destined to become the largest in the nation by 1970. *Eight* more Congressional seats are to be added in 1960, the increase alone being larger than the entire delegation in more than half of the states. Not only does this bring growing external pressure upon the state, but it aggravates the perennially partisan question of legislative districting. The "decennial gerrymander" takes on new meaning in terms of party conflict in a state which has witnessed the number of congressmen increase by 60 per cent in twenty years.

Against this back drop of increasing two-party competition, important state problems wait to be solved. Perhaps the most pressing is the question of water development, centering on consideration of a 1,750,000,000-dollar bond issue. This question has already brought to the surface the most enduring conflict in California's domestic politics, the contest for influence and power between North and South: the water-hungry South, dependent on imported water for its continued expansion, indeed, its present survival, with a growing preponderance of the state's population; the water-rich North, demanding a guarantee of its future water rights, and forced to rely for protection on a rurally dominated state senate. Threats to return the state senate to a population base (abandoned in 1926) have featured the Southern campaign against the reluctant Northerners.

The contest between North and South is not in the traditional up-state versus down-state, rural versus urban mold that is characteristic of state and local politics in other parts of the country. Both sections of the state are important agriculturally, both contain large metropolitan centers, both are highly urbanized, both are relatively equal in the distribution of party strength. In addition, both rural and urban areas of the state are similar in the political character of their population. Farm counties contain proportionately as many Democrats as the large cities.[4] These factors have led to a blurring, although not the complete absence, of rural-urban political competition. The charge is not widely leveled in California, as it is in New York, for example, that the metropolitan areas are supporting the rural local governments through state subsidies and grants-in-aid.[5]

The existence of a single League of California Cities, that includes all farm as well as metropolitan centers in its membership is a factor in this regard. While the largest cities maintain their own lobbyists in Sacramento, the league's position of speaking for all cities in the state, regardless of size, has an important influence. On the other hand, the league is able to bring urban needs and pressures to bear upon rural legislators by its representation of small towns. To a lesser degree, the County Supervisors' Association plays the same role.

THE LOCAL SCENE

In 1957, there were 3,878 local government units in California. These included the 57 counties and one city-county (San Francisco), 330 incorporated cities, 1,840 school districs, and 1,650 special districts covering almost every aspect of local govern-

---

[4] With respect to several social characteristics, Key notes "the fairly consistent similarities between California metropolitan and nonmetropolitan populations, in contrast with the wider differences between these populations in other states, and the deviate character of the California party system." Key, *American State Politics: An Introduction* (1956), p. 240.

[5] See, for example, Vidich and Bensman, *Small Town in Mass Society* (1958), pp. 198–202.

ment.[6] By 1960, the number of cities had increased to 362, continuing the trend of the 1950's. From 1935 to 1955, the number of cities grew by 34, but in the mere five years from 1955 to 1960, by 47. This was primarily the result, of course, of the impact of population growth, but also of a system of shared revenues between the state and the cities making it economically feasible for communities to support local units of government adequately.

Legally, a California city may be a small village with a population of less than 1,000 or a metropolitan center of several millions. All incorporated communities in the state are classed as "cities," regardless of size, and an area with a population of 500 or more is eligible to initiate incorporation proceedings. More than half of the state's cities have a population of less than 10,000, only 5 per cent of more than 100,000. In addition to incorporated cities, there are many urban centers in the state, including communities of up to 40,000, which are primarily governed by the county and classed as unincorporated territories.

Against this general background, three points concerning California municipalities make a study of local politics of special interest: home rule, the council-manager plan, and the nonpartisan system of elections.

Home Rule.—While no objective standard has been developed to measure the degree of a state's home rule, California cities probably enjoy the greatest municipal independence in the nation. This is true both in law and in actual practice, as a result of constitutional language, favorable court action, and a militant League of Cities which has successfully persuaded the legislature not to encroach unduly on what the league considers essential municipal powers.

For example, California's charter cities (any city of more than 3,500 may adopt a charter, and there were 70 such municipalities in 1960) are free to adopt any local tax not expressly prohibited by the state constitution or the city's own charter. No specific legislative enactment is required. This springs from the fact that, while in most states cities must find express or directly implied legislative language as a basis for some particular program, California charter cities are free to take any action in "municipal affairs" not

---

[6] U.S. Department of Commerce, Bureau of the Census, *U.S. Census of Governments: 1957,* I, 14.

expressly prohibited by the constitution or the local charter. California's general-law or noncharter cities have been able to obtain almost as great a measure of local autonomy through successful legislative action as have the generally larger cities through the adoption of home-rule charters.

Council-Manager Government.—Related to the extent of local autonomy and to the large number of newly incorporated cities in recent years, both the council-manager and council-administrative-officer plans are more widely employed in California than in most other states, and the appointed-executive system is highly popular. Two-thirds of the cities employ a manager or administrative officer, and most of the remaining communities have a population of less than 5,000.

Because of the prevalence of this form of city government, a study of California local politics must be concerned with the relationships between the form of government and the political context in which it is placed, a subject of special importance in view of the rapid growth of council-manager government throughout the nation.

The Nonpartisan Ballot.—All California local officials—city, county, or district—are elected under a nonpartisan system in which party labels do not appear on the ballot nor are party-nominating primaries employed. Therefore, and because of the past weakness of the party system generally, the state provides probably as "pure" an example as possible of the effect of the absence of formalized local party structure.

The extent to which California cities, under their constitutional or statutory home-rule powers, have authority to alter their election system is not absolutely clear. An opinion of the state's attorney general, stimulated by the writer and delivered in 1956, holds that the related questions of the adoption of a partisan primary election as a nominating mechanism for municipal officers or a requirement that the party affiliation of local candidates appear on the ballot are matters of local concern.[7] While the opinion makes evident the absence of clear precedent for its findings, it suggests that in charter cities either or both measures could be adopted by action of the city council if not prohibited by the city charter. Alternatively, either could be adopted by amend-

---

[7] California, Attorney General, *Opinions* No. 55/184 (April 18, 1956).

ment to the city charter if the city council lacked the power it-self to provide for such changes. With reference to general-law cities, the opinion holds that the legislature may provide for a partisan ballot and a partisan primary by appropriate amendments to the *Elections Code* and that such a provision may be made mandatory for all general-law cities or may "probably" be made permissive, to be effective only on action of the local city council.

Somewhat different conclusions with reference to counties of the state are contained in the opinion.

No information readily exists to indicate the extent to which the ballot form would be regarded as a matter of "local concern" elsewhere in the nation. As suggested, California's tradition of home rule is very thorough-going, and in other states other con-stitutional bars to local control of elections might well exist. In California, the form of municipal elections appears to be a subject of popular control of the local council or electorate or the legisla-ture and is not—as far as the form of ballot is concerned at least—limited by the state's constitution.

The Metropolitan Problem.—Of the many problems facing California cities, none seems as pressing as the question of metro-politan government. Of the 362 cities in 1960, 83 were found in the nine-county San Francisco Bay Area, another 67 in Los An-geles County alone. Already coöperating in a variety of programs —the most important being water, rapid transit, and air-pollution control—citizens of these and other metropolitan areas in the state (such as Fresno, Sacramento, and San Diego) are asking themselves what the future pattern of local government should be. A special gubernatorial commission, appointed in 1959, is hoping to provide an adequate answer.

RECAPITULATION

Here is California in 1960: Its area larger than Italy, Germany, or Japan and comprising a wide diversity in topography, climate, and natural resources; its population soon to be the most numerous in the nation, largely urban and metropolitan, and including mil-lions of persons with a background and experience gained in other states; its state government facing problems of unprecedented magnitude in the maintenance of a sound economy and the provision of public services to a citizenry increasing by more than one thousand each day; its political parties dramatically changing from traditional weakness to increasing strength.

In this dynamic environment, the politics of California cities take place. These communities range in size from villages of fewer than 1,000 to Los Angeles, with 2,450,000 inhabitants. Regardless of size, all California municipalities enjoy a large measure of home rule. Almost all California cities with a population of more than 5,000 employ the council-manager or some other appointed-executive-officer system; the plan enjoys a popularity as great as anywhere in the nation. The nonpartisan ballot is universally employed for local elections although there apears to be no constitutional bar to the adoption of a partisan ballot or primary at the city level. In addition to the panoply of normal municipal problems in a period of growth, the citizens of California are facing the question of how to govern the metropolitan region.

3

Nonpartisanship 1760–1960

Key

THE DEFINITION OF THE NONPARTISAN FORM OF ELECTIONS is similar to that which might be offered to describe the legal form of the nomination and election of members of the British Parliament: nomination by simple petition and a ballot free from party labels. And yet, the British election system is most often cited as highly partisan. Thus, a distinction must be made between the form of balloting and the political environment in which the balloting takes place. Theoretically, the scale used to describe the electoral process might include a thoroughly partisan context in which a nonpartisan ballot was employed or a thoroughly nonpartisan context in which a partisan ballot was employed, and

doubtless, examples could be found to fit these extremes. Throughout this study, nonpartisan—unless otherwise qualified—refers to
the *form* of elections and not to the political environment or state
of mind. It is the origin of the nonpartisan form of election that is
of concern here.

A CAPSULE HISTORY OF THE NONPARTISAN BALLOT

The development of the nonpartisan ballot is a chapter in the
general history of nomination and election procedures in the
United States.[1] As Carl Bridenbaugh indicates, this history com-
mences appropriately enough in a "smoke-filled room" in the
colonial period where candidates were "nominated" for local office by informal caucuses. He writes that in 1763 "John Adams
discovered how 'a clique of intriguers' managed things":

> This day learned that the Caucus Club meets, at certain
> times, in the garret of Tom Dawes, the Adjutant of the
> Boston Regiment. He has a large house, and he has a
> movable partition in his garret which he takes down, and
> the whole club meets in one room. There they smoke tobacco,
> till you cannot see from one end of the garret to the other.
> There they drink flip, I suppose, and there they choose a
> moderator, who puts questions to the vote regularly; and
> selectmen, assessors, collectors, wardens, firewards, and re-
> presentatives, are regularly chosen before they are chosen
> in the town. . . . They send committees to wait on the
> merchant's club, and to propose and join in the choice of
> men and measures.[2]

That these activities could be successful, as in a later day, is indicated by Bridenbaugh's finding that in the period from 1760 to

---

[1] Except where reference is made to specific quotations, the material included
in the following brief discussion of historical origins of the nonpartisan electoral
system has been derived from the following sources: Albright, *The American
Ballot* (1942); Anderson, *American City Government* (1925); Cushman, "Nonpartisan Nominations and Elections," *Annals of the American Academy of Political
and Social Science* CVI (March, 1923), pp. 83–96; Munro, *Municipal Government and Administration* (1923); Penniman, *Sait's American Parties and Elections*
(5th ed., rev., 1952). Material with specific reference to California is derived from:
Cresap, *Party Politics in the Golden State* (1954); Crouch *et. al.*, *California
Government and Politics* (1956).

[2] Bridenbaugh, *Cities in Revolt: Urban Life in America, 1743–1776* (1955). pp.
221–222.

1775, "the Caucus and Merchant's Club so managed elections that their men won out regularly." [3]

With the limited extent of the suffrage and the relatively small size of the communities, such nominating procedures were apparently adequate for the day. The elections for borough and city offices were equally informal by present-day standards. The choice of candidates was made by such methods as a show of hands, a "corn and bean ballot" (where each candidate was voted on separately by means of colored beans until one had a majority) or by an oral statement at the polls. These local elections were held on days separate from those on which colonial and then state balloting took place.

Informal as these procedures were, they served as vehicles for active politics.

> Within each city [from 1740 to 1770] the inhabitants divided over social and economic questions, into the many and few. They did not have the elaborate machinery and carefully framed programs of a later day; rather did they split into unorganized 'factions' when contentions spread. Nevertheless these party beginnings are of great importance, and contemporaries recognized them for what they were.[4]

With the growth of cities, the expansion of the electorate, and the increase in political party activity, the electoral process began to change in the early nineteenth century. Informal party meetings developed into a formal, but entirely extralegal, system of ward caucuses at which candidates for district office were nominated and delegates selected to a city convention at which city-wide candidates were chosen to carry the party banner. This system of municipal nominations continued to be used in most American cities until the end of the nineteenth century. Munro indicates that, "in some cities it was the custom, however, to hold a 'citizens' caucus' to which members of all political parties were admitted. This caucus made nominations without reference to the party affiliations of the candidates." [5] Gradually, as the party organizations strove to gain public office at every governmental level, the move was also advanced to have all elections held on

---

[3] *Ibid.*, p. 222.
[4] *Ibid.*, p. 12.
[5] Munro, *op. cit.*, I, 260.

the same day. The earlier methods of voting were gradually re-
placed by a paper ballot, written or printed, and provided by the
candidate, the party, or the individual voter. Party ballots were
usually printed in distinctive colors or with distinguishing em-
blems. To permit split-ticket voting, individual candidates or
slates often prepared gummed stickers which could be pasted
over the names of those on the regular party ballot. Frequently
one party counterfeited the ballots of another, or ballots were
prepared joining the candidates of the various parties in a variety
of combinations.

The resulting confusion led to reforms of the nominating procedure and the ballot. California was one of the first states to
adopt an optional law regulating political caucuses. This measure,
enacted in 1866, could be adopted voluntarily by any political
association which wished to invoke its protection and called for
full notice to be given by the party of the time and place of
nominating caucuses. Similar measures in other states required,
for example, that such meetings be limited to regular members
of the party and that votes be counted honestly.

At the same time, ballot reform was continued. In 1872 California required that all parties print their ballot on paper furn-
ished by the state, uniform in weight, texture, and color. Oregon
adopted a similar law at about the same time, and other states
followed.

However, not until 1888, more than fifteen years later, was the
so-called Australian ballot, printed and distributed at state expense, required in an American election. The first such measure
was enacted by the Kentucky legislature and applied only to the
Louisville municipal election, voice voting being prescribed at
the time for all other elections in the state. The law provided that
all candidates who presented a petition of fifty signatures could
be placed on the ballot in alphabetical order below the title of
the appropriate office. No party designation appeared on the ballot, so that it may be said that the first officially printed ballot
employed in the United States was a nonpartisan ballot. As
Cushman suggests: "The nonpartisan feature of this law can
hardly be attributed, however, to an appreciation of the problem
[of the proper role of the party in the election process]." [6]

---

[6] Cushman, *op. cit.*, p. 84.

It was more likely, rather, that the Kentucky legislature simply adopted the ballot form as it had been developed in Australia and Britain. However, voters faced with the task of filling a dozen or more offices under the typical long ballot of the day were "utterly helpless" when confronted with long lists of names, unidentified as to party affiliation or endorsement. To meet this problem, the Massachusetts law adopted in 1888 and applied to all cities of the state provided that the party designation of the officially nominated candidates appear on the ballot following his name. For the first time, a legal definition of a political party was required; the law described party as an organization casting a certain percentage of the aggregate vote and recognized party nominations when certified by the presiding officer of the convention or caucus. Independent candidates might also be nominated by petition as under the Louisville procedure. The Massachusetts measure was followed closely in the act adopted in California in 1891. By the presidential elections of 1882, Brooks reports, thirty-two states had provided for an Australian ballot.[7]

With the Australian ballot in general use, the concentration of the reformers shifted to increased regulation of the nominating conventions. For example, following several false starts by the legislature which were ruled unconstitutional, California voters in 1900 amended the state constitution to empower the legislature to regulate the election of delegates to nominating conventions. The resulting act of 1901 provided for a comprehensive system of primary elections for delegates to conventions at local, district, and state levels at which candidates for office, from councilman to governor, would be nominated.

However, the convention—even thoroughly regulated—proved to be in its last days in many states including California. Wisconsin was the first state to adopt a state-wide direct primary law, superseding the convention system and providing for the direct choice of party candidates by the general electorate of the two parties. Other states quickly followed her example, California in 1909.

Concurrently, a separate measure was being initiated at the local level, the *nonpartisan* primary election, a plan of nominations and elections resembling the Louisville system of 1888. Candidates for city office were nominated by petition and appeared

---

[7] Brooks, *Political Parties and Electoral Problems*, 3d ed., rev. (1933), p. 272.

on the ballot without party designation. In some cases, as the plan developed, the highest two candidates for each office in the initial or primary election would compete in a final or runoff contest, again with no party label on the ballot. In some instances a candidate gaining a clear majority in the primary would be declared elected without having to stand in a runoff. Or, as the plan came to be practiced in most California cities, the primary disappeared altogether, only one election was held, and plurality victories became common.

Two other measures, parallel to the nonpartisan election and motivated by similar considerations, were advanced simultaneously by the reformers. The first was to separate the date of the city election from that at which state and national officers were chosen, either by holding the municipal contests in the spring or in odd-numbered years. This proposal had already been long discussed and apparently adopted in many cities, although the partisan ballot was still maintained. The second reform, essential if nonpartisan elections were to be at all feasible, was the short ballot. Advocates of this movement proposed that the host of elected administrative officials so common in the typical city of the day be made appointive, that remaining bicameral city councils be consolidated, and that the number of councilmen be reduced. The commission plan of city government met all these goals, and it was not surprising that the first reported return to the nonpartisan ballot was accomplished with the adoption of the Dallas city charter of 1907, which provided for the commission form. Reed points out: "Nothing was said of nonpartisanship or the presence of party designation on the ballot, a situation easily explicable in view of the overwhelming dominance of the Democratic Party." [8] In the same year, South Dakota and Iowa provided for the optional adoption of a similar system of government and elections by cities of these two states, the nonpartisan ballot being specifically described in these statutes.

Boston, in 1909, appears to have been the first large American community to remove the party designation from the municipal ballot. In the same year Berkeley became the initial California city to abolish the party convention as the method of nominating local officials, when it too amended its charter to provide for a

---

[8] Reed, *Municipal Government in the United States*, 2d ed., rev. (1943), p. 193.

nonpartisan ballot and nomination by petition. Other California cities quickly followed suit.

In 1911, California applied the nonpartisan ballot to elected school officials, and in 1913, the system was extended to include county, township, and general-law (noncharter) city officials. It is not known whether any California charter cities attempted to continue the partisan designation on the ballot after this date, but the evidence would suggest that none did. By 1914, Griffith states, the nonpartisan primary and ballot "were incorporated in the majority of new charters [in the United States]," [9] and state legislatures adopted similar legislation for noncharter cities.

Paralleling this effort to remove the partisan designation from the ballot at the municipal level was a drive to bring the election of judges under the nonpartisan system. This was accomplished in California and Arizona in 1911, and other states soon followed.

In 1913, through a series of circumstances unrelated to ballot reform, Minnesota adopted the nonpartisan ballot for members of the legislature and has continued to employ the system for those officers until this day.[10] The California legislature went even further in 1915 in providing that all elective state offices be made nonpartisan, but in a referendum held in October, 1915, the action was defeated by the voters 156,967 to 112,681. Subsequently, North Dakota voters defeated a similar measure in 1924, while Nebraska applied the nonpartisan ballot to state legislators in 1935 after having defeated the proposal in 1924.

No central source provides information on the extent of the current use of the nonpartisan ballot in the various local elections of the fifty states.[11] In summary it can be said only that the non-

---

[9] Griffith, *The Modern Development of City Government in the United Kingdom and the United States* (1927), p. 271.

[10] See Charles R. Adrian, "The Nonpartisan Legislature in Minnesota" (1950).

[11] In 1950, Adrian (*ibid.*, p. 311) reported that seventeen states choose some or all of their judiciary without party designation, and that nearly one-half of the nation's population elects various local officials by this method. He reported that California, Minnesota, and North Dakota elect virtually all local officials by this means. Penniman, in 1952, indicated that sixteen states apply the principle to judicial office, eleven of the sixteen being in the Pacific, Mountain, and West Central regions. He reported also that three states have extended the practice to all county offices: California, North Dakota, and Minnesota; and nine states to school office. See *Sait's American Politics and Elections* 5th ed., rev. (1952), pp. 369, 371. A *National Municipal Review* editorial in May, 1951 (p. 241) partly corroborated this report and stated that in most counties outside of California, Minnesota, and North Dakota, elections are "still tied in fact to the fortunes and rivalries of the national parties." However, Childs amends the Penniman state-

partisan ballot is used primarily to elect schoolboard members, city councilmen, and mayors in a large number of local governments, a far lesser number of county officials, members of the judiciary in approximately one-third of the states, and members of the state legislature in Minnesota and Nebraska. Adrian estimates that "the total number of offices filled by this method is probably equal to more than one-half of the total number in the United States." [12]

Facts concerning the use of the nonpartisan ballot in city elections are more readily available, however. Table 1 shows the increase in use of the system in the last quarter-century. The earliest report in 1929 indicates that in approximately 57 per cent of the cities with a population of more than 30,000 the party designation did not appear on the local ballot. Thirty years later, the nearest comparable figure (for all cities of more than 25,000) was 65 per cent. While the proportionate increase in the number of nonpartisan cities has not been great, the number of cities with nonpartisan elections increased by 56 per cent from 1940 to 1959. Today, most cities of all sizes use the nonpartisan ballot, most frequently the cities in the 250,000–499,999 range.

The nonpartisan form of election is most frequently found in council-manager cities—84 per cent of all cities with a population of more than 5,000, as compared to but 44 per cent of the mayor-council cities and 62 per cent of the commission cities.

As table 2 shows, this relationship exists regardless of the size of city. In fact, the large manager cities are more frequently non-

---

ment as far as school boards are concerned and reports that 86 per cent of the elected school boards in the United States are chosen in nonpartisan elections. See *Civic Victories* (1952), p. 219. Bromage's text of 1950 cites California, Missouri, Minnesota, North Dakota, Ohio, Washington, and Wisconsin as requiring a nonpartisan ballot for all cities. See *Introduction to Municipal Government and Administration* (1950), p. 221. An examination of the *Municipal Yearbook's* listing of the type of ballot employed in each city with a population of more than 25,000 indicated a slightly different pattern as of 1959. In the following eighteen states, no city of this size or larger employed a partisan ballot: Alaska, California, Colorado, Florida, Idaho, Kansas, Minnesota, Nebraska, Nevada, New Hampshire, North Dakota, Oregon, South Dakota, Tennessee, Utah, Washington, Wisconsin, and Wyoming. In five states, no city of 25,000 or more employed a nonpartisan ballot: Delaware, Hawaii, Indiana, Pennsylvania, and Vermont. The remaining states included at least one city using each type of ballot. See International City Managers' Association, *The Municipal Yearbook, 1959* (1959), pp. 89–99; information for Hawaii received from the governor's office.

---

[12] Adrian, "A Typology for Nonpartisan Elections," *Western Political Quarterly*, XII (June, 1959), 449.

TABLE 1

U.S. Cities with a Nonpartisan Ballot for Municipal Elections, 1929-1959

Class	1929a			1934a			1940			1950			1959		
	Total number of cities	Number non-partisan	Per cent non-partisan	Total number of cities	Number non-partisan	Per cent non-partisan	Total number of cities	Number non-partisan	Per cent non-partisan	Total number of cities	Number non-partisan	Per cent non-partisan	Total number of cities	Number non-partisan	Per cent non-partisan
By form of government															
Mayor-council	142	95	67.0	155	60	39.0	1,116	451	40.4	1,160	486	41.9	1,235	543	44.0
Commission	82	64	78.0	79	60	76.0	307	235	76.5	298	224	75.1	306	190	62.1
Council-manager	60	51	85.0	69	59	85.0	302	263	87.1	492	399	81.1	909	764	84.0
Town meeting	0	0	0	0	0	0	54	0	0	47	34	72.3	45	24	53.3
Representative town meeting	0	0	0	0	0	0	27	0	0	26	18	69.2	25	20	80.0
By population															
More than 500,000	13	7	61.5	13	8	61.5	13	7	53.8	13	6	46.2	17	11	64.7
250,000-499,999	23	19	82.6	23	17	73.9	23	17	73.9	22	18	81.8	23	19	82.6
100,000-249,999	57	28	49.1	56	30	53.5	56	34	60.7	55	34	61.8	68	40	58.8
50,000-99,999	94	55	58.5	98	59	60.2	98	61	62.2	105	61	58.1	132	95	72.0
25,000-49,999	95b	52b	54.7	119b	67b	56.3	177	102	57.6	207	131	63.3	289	179	61.9
10,000-24,999	0	0	0	0	0	0	592	317	53.5	661	373	56.4	833	516	61.9
5,000-9,999	0	0	0	0	0	0	847	466	55.0	960	556	57.9	1,158	706	61.0
TOTALc	282	161	57.1	309	181	58.6	1,806	1,004	55.6	2,023	1,179	58.3	2,520	1,566	62.1

a Reports data only for cities over 30,000. In 1934, more than 90 per cent of the 320 council-manager cities *less than* 30,000 population reporting (out of a possible total of 364) conducted nonpartisan council elections.

b 30,000-49,999.

c Number of cities in column sometimes varies from total due to selective omission of several small cities and to inadequacies of reported data.

SOURCE: International City Managers' Association, *Municipal Year Book, 1959*, p. 84; *1950*, p. 43; *1940*, pp. 23, 28-60; *1934*, pp. 102, 107-112. Detroit Bureau of Governmental Research, *The Form of Government in 288 American Cities* No. 121 (February, 1931), pp. 4, 11-15.

partisan than the smaller, in contrast to expectations. Similarly, although the pattern is mixed, the larger mayor-council cities are more likely to be nonpartisan in their form of elections than the smaller cities.

TABLE 2

FORM OF GOVERNMENT AND FORM OF ELECTIONS
(Mayor-Council and Council-Manager Cities Only)

	Total number of cities	Council-Manager				Mayor-Council			
		Partisan		Nonpartisan		Partisan		Nonpartisan	
Size of city		Number	Per cent	Number	Per cent	Number	Per cent	Number	Per cent
500,000 and more	17	0	0	1	100	6	38	10	62
250,000-499,999	18	1	11	8	89	3	33	6	67
100,000-249,999	55	3	12	23	88	19	66	10	34
50,000-99,999	106	8	13	53	87	19	42	26	58
25,000-49,999	238	23	17	112	83	66	64	37	36
TOTAL	434	35	15	197	85	113	56	89	44

SOURCE: *Municipal Yearbook 1959*

The form of elections, partisan or nonpartisan, is also related to two other aspects of local government: the directly-elected versus the council-appointed mayor and ward versus at-large election of councilmen. Of cities with a population of more than 25,000 and using partisan elections, 89 per cent also elect their mayor directly as contrasted with only 56 per cent of the nonpartisan cities. Reversing the figures, 45 per cent of cities with a directly elected mayor are partisan whereas only 11 per cent of appointed-mayor cities are partisan. Almost all mayor-council cities directly elect the mayor regardless of ballot form or size of city. However, of the nonpartisan-manager cities only 36 per cent have a directly elected mayor, while 63 per cent of partisan-manager cities elect their chief executive. As table 3 suggests, this relationship exists regardless of size of city, except for the ten manager cities with a population of more than 250,000.

The relationship is equally marked with reference to at-large versus ward elections. In 25 per cent of the cities with partisan elections all councilmen are elected at-large, but 62 per cent of the nonpartisan cities elect all legislators in this fashion. Put in other terms, 83 per cent of the at-large cities are nonpartisan as contrasted with only 50 per cent of the cities using the ward system, either exclusively or in combination. Regardless of the size of city, nonpartisan communities are more likely to use the

at-large system exclusively whereas partisan cities are far more
likely to elect at least some of the council by wards. The pattern
for cities using *only* the ward system is mixed. Only one partisan

TABLE 3

PARTISAN ELECTIONS AND THE DIRECT ELECTION
OF THE MAYOR IN COUNCIL-MANAGER CITIES

	Partisan			Nonpartisan		
		Directly elected mayor			Directly elected mayor	
Size of City	Number of cities	Number	Per cent	Number of cities	Number	Per cent
500,000 and more	0	0	0	1	0	0
250,000-499,999	1	0	0	8	4	50
100,000-249,999	3	3	100	23	9	39
50,000- 99,999	8	6	75	53	18	34
25,000- 49,999	23	13	57	112	40	36
TOTAL	35	22	63	197	71	36

SOURCE: *Municipal Yearbook 1959*

city of more than 250,000 uses the ward system exclusively,
whereas seven nonpartisan cities do so. Below the quarter-million
population range, however, the all-ward elections are relatively
much more frequent in partisan cities than in nonpartisan cities
as table 4 demonstrates.

TABLE 4

PARTISAN ELECTIONS AND AT-LARGE OR WARD ELECTIONS
(Mayor-Council and Council-Manager Cities Only)

	Partisan				Nonpartisan			
	Number of cities	Per cent of cities			Number of cities	Per cent of cities		
Size of City		At-large	Ward	Combination		At-large	Ward	Combination
500,000 and more	6	17	17	66	11	36	46	18
250,000-499,999	4	50	0	50	14	72	14	14
100,000-249,999	22	23	41	36	33	76	9	15
50,000- 99,999	27	37	33	30	79	61	18	21
25,000- 49,999	87	22	41	37	148	61	18	21
TOTAL	146	25	38	37	285	62	18	20

SOURCE: *Municipal Yearbook 1959*

THE RATIONALE OF NONPARTISANSHIP

The roots of the nonpartisan system of nominations and elections lie deep in the history of the Reform and Progressive period. Adrian has summarized the basis for the movement:

> [The reform movement in state and local government] was inspired by the example of the success of the corporate structure in the business world, coupled with a revulsion against the low standards of morality to be found in many places in the "great game of politics" around the turn of the century. The contemporary brand of politician had recently been exposed by the "muckrakers" and the prestige of the political party had reached a very low level. Using the basic assumptions that (1) the political party and politicians in general were not to be trusted and (2) the principles of "efficient business administration" could and should be applied to democratic government, the great reform movement that centered in the second decade of the twentieth century urged, in various degrees of intensity in various parts of the nation, all or part of the following: the primary election, proportional representation, a shorter ballot, concentration of responsibility in state administrative structure, the unicameral legislature, council-manager and commission government in cities, the initiative, referendum and recall, and the nonpartisan election of certain public officials.[13]

With specific reference to the closely related issues of (1) the separation of the date of city elections from that at which state or national officials were chosen and (2) the adoption of the nonpartisan ballot for local offices, the following arguments were put forth by the nonpartisan advocates.[14]

City government is largely a matter of "good business

---

[13] Adrian, "The Nonpartisan Legislature in Minnesota" (1950), p. 5.

[14] The distinction was not always made clear as to whether the evil to be avoided was partisanship per se or partisanship based on *national* party lines. Some nonpartisan advocates appear to have been arguing generally against any political organization, even though purely local in character, whereas others—probably in the majority—merely argued against the intrusion of national partisanship into the local scene.

practice" or, as Clarence Ludwig has recently put it, "municipal housekeeping." [15] The problems and issues that come before a city council are not really political, and the role of "politics" is small.

Party labels are associated in people's minds with national issues (in that day the tariff and currency matters were most frequently cited as examples), and these ought not to be the basis for selecting local officials. Said Frank Goodnow in 1900: "City government must, to be efficient, be emancipated from the tyranny of the national and State political parties." [16] The political parties have never developed meaningful programs at the local level; the nonpartisan system emphasizes and highlights local issues which should feature the election of a mayor or councilman and, subsequently, the vote of these officials on questions of public policy. The voter must be set free from the "entangling web of inherited traditions" when he casts his ballot for local candidates. Although simply removing the label from the ballot does not remove partisanship from the local scene, it reduces party influence and promotes independence.

The evils of the machine, the boss, and the spoils system require that all "good" citizens, regardless of party, combine in the interests of good government, and the nonpartisan ballot will aid in this move. The nonpartisan ballot promotes the strength of independent civic associations.[17]

The political parties will never be meaningful and useful instruments on the state and national scene as long as they must concern themselves with the minutiae of local government and be subject to the temptation of local spoils and patronage. [A related but unique view is that a ballot free from party designation is to be desired because it removes the party from legal regulation and gives it independence to

---

[15] Ludwig, "No Place for Parties," *National Civic Review*, XLVIII (May, 1959), 237.

[16] In National Municipal League, *A Municipal Program* (1900), pp. 144–145. The emphasis on "efficiency" is significant.

[17] Paradoxically, the nonpartisan movement could also be used to promote the cause of a political boss. It would appear that one of the reasons behind Tom Pendergast's support of the St. Louis "reform" charter of 1925 was his belief that he could better withstand a nation-wide Republican trend if the ballot was freed from party labels. See, for example, Brown, *The Politics of Reform: Kansas City's Municipal Government, 1925–1950* (1958).

nominate candidates as it wishes and otherwise to pursue its own ways.[18]]

Better candidates can be recruited for local office if they do not have to fight their way through the party machines to get there. Members of the national party which is in a minority in the city can still play their full role as participating citizens in the work of their city government under the nonpartisan system.

As cities gain independence from the state through the extension of home rule, the need for political ties is reduced and the possibility of "political home rule" (i.e., local or independent parties and candidates) is made more feasible. Similarly, the extension of the short ballot makes the nonpartisan election practical.

Parties are unable to promote group responsibility for candidates and programs in the city hall, as can also be seen by the fact that such responsibility has never really existed at either the state or national levels of government. Local responsibility becomes possible when attention can be focused on community issues and programs as under the nonpartisan system.

These and other arguments were used successfully by the California proponents of the nonpartisan ballot, and, by 1913, all local government officials and judges in the state were elected without formal reference to party labels. The general campaign of the Hiram Johnson Progressives against the Southern Pacific machine and the disclosures of Boss Abe Ruef's San Francisco activities were highlights in the history of the "reformers." Of special note was the relationship between the city machine and the state's political structure revealed in Ruef's attempts at maneuvering within the Republican state convention in 1906.

Suggestive of the attitudes of the Progressives is this description of the San Francisco scene in the early 1900's:

> Under the provisions of our charter, as it existed prior to 1910, the following objectionable results obtained: (1) The selection of candidates for office nominated by party conventions dictated and controlled by political bosses. (2) A partisan rather than an efficient administration of municipal

---

[18] Penniman, *op. cit.*, p. 371.

affairs. . . . The old municipal nominating convention, like the county and state conventions, with their boss-chosen and boss-controlled delegates, had become intolerable; while partisan government based upon a so-called party responsibility was demonstrated to be another name for boss rule applied to the administration of the office itself.[19]

The National Municipal League.—Since the first meeting of the National Municipal League in 1894, the battle for the nonpartisan ballot and related elements of the reform platform has been most consistently carried by the league. Today, its journal and its publications serve as the main vehicles for advocacy of the movement. Its views parallel those of the original nonpartisan sponsors, but, in addition, new arguments have been added. For example, in 1953, a league publication stated that

> the intervention of the national parties in municipal affairs typically has either or both of two undesirable effects: 1. It overrides and obscures the real local issues and keeps them from being given effective consideration, and/or 2. It injects irrelevant considerations of local patronage and personal ambition into the national party counsels and thus tends to depreciate both the integrity and the clarity of national politics.[20]

Evidence is given, in the league's opinion, to contradict the notion that "national parties cannot live without local party mercenaries [who participate in municipal politics]."

In a second place is noted the "close connection between the fight to free municipal politics from the control of the national parties and effective municipal home rule," while in another area, the document attacks the "beguiling" but "superficial" argument that the growth of intergovernmental relations necessitates intergovernmental political activity by the two parties. "The fact is, of course," states the report, "that inter-governmental programs are largely worked out and conducted at the professional, not the party, level and that many of these programs have substantial

---

[19] Jordan *in* "Municipal Elections," Commonwealth Club of California *Transactions*, XI (August, 1916), 179.

[20] National Municipal League, *Getting the National Parties Out of Municipal Elections* (July, 1953), (mimeographed). All quotations in this and the following paragraph are from pages 1 and 2 of this report.

support in both parties." But even if this not be the case, the league argues in an attempt to cover all contingencies—even if contradictory, city councils under the nonpartisan system "commonly" have members of both parties within their membership, and this fact aids political contact with the state house or Congress, regardless of which party may be in control at these levels. The introductory text of this report, which precedes the compilation of excerpts, concludes with the view that under the nonpartisan system "it is generally easier for wholesome independent action to occur."

The leading nonpartisan advocate of the league over the years has been Richard Childs, currently chairman of its executive committee. In his book, *Civic Victories,* he calls for a system of elections which will make it feasible for the people to put into public office the *individual man* they really want.[21] This necessitates, of course, the short ballot. It is also, states Childs, "a matter of exposing candidates to adequate public examination before election, so that when the voters go to the polls they will have had ample information to enable them to decide which man they want as their representative servant." He expresses his confidence that "the voter can accumulate and carry in his head his brief list of personal preferences and do without guidance of party names and symbols on the ballot." In voting "blindly" for a party ticket, "the people are simply delegating their choice to a few half-known, possibly irresponsible men whom they had no voice in choosing. . . . This is not democracy, but oligarchy." In accepting even the most honestly devised ticket, either under a partisan or nonpartisan system, Childs asserts, the voters are allowing "sets of candidates to be tied together for them in bunches like asparagus and then [they] vote for them by the bunch." This criticism of action which would tend to introduce any sort of group between the voter and the individual candidate is later modified. Under conditions of the short-ballot and nonpartisan elections, "a committee of citizens who have no private ax to grind and whose ability and selflessness are widely recognized can . . . exert a wholesome influence by providing a little timely leadership."

---

[21] Childs, *Civic Victories* (1952). The quotations to follow are from pages 11–13, 299, 301.

Many such statements are repeated in the league's recent publication, *Model County Charter*.[22] But there is evidence in the introduction to this document of an increasing understanding that the problem is not simple. It is recognized that the voters may actually "choose" to divide along national party lines in their local political actions and that there are many examples of local officials of high caliber being elected under a partisan system. Furthermore, a revitalization of county politics essential to citizen control "can in some areas be encouraged by action to make the national parties more responsible and genuinely competitive in their approaches to county affairs." On the other hand, John Bebout, the author of the introduction, notes the large number of counties "where there is no genuine contest between or within the parties, with the result that the people are subjected to one party government in the name of the national two-party system." He observes, also, the frequency of the tendency to submerge important issues of good county government in appeals for party unity in the interest of state and national political success, and, contrastingly, that forced local activity may divert the local party organizations from their primary task "of serving the voters as instrumentalities for expression of genuine differences over national and state policies and leadership."

But, concludes Bebout in a statement significant for an official league document:

> The decision as to the best method of electing the county council, including the question of what part if any the national parties should play, is not a simple one. It should be made in each case in the light of a hard-headed analysis of the particular needs and traditions of the county and the nature and adaptability of the existing political pattern. The *Model* does not presume to provide the answer; it does offer ways in which different answers appropriate to different counties may be written into their charters.[23]

However, a still later publication refuses to apply this more flexible position to the cities of the nation and returns to the traditional league position: "National and state parties have no

---

[22] National Municipal League, *Model County Charter* (1956). The quotations to follow are from pages xxv–xxvii.

[23] *Ibid.*, p. xxvii.

valid significance in municipal affairs and it has proved unfor-
tunate to have municipal elections decided solely upon the basis
of electing Democrats or Republicans." [24]

Robert Wood ably summarizes the basic philosophy behind
these arguments in support of the nonpartisan system, past and
present:

> Finally, and most fundamentally, no-party politics implies
> some positive assumptions about political behavior that go
> beyond simple antagonism to partisanship. Inescapably,
> there is a belief that the individual can and should arrive
> at his political convictions untutored and unled; and expecta-
> tion that in the formal process of election and decision mak-
> ing a consensus will emerge through the process of right
> reason and by the higher call to the common good . . . the
> citizen, on his own, knows best. . . .
>
> As a theory, nonpartisanship harks back to the traditional
> concept of local government, to Jefferson's high expectations
> for the rational capacity of the yeoman, and to that strand
> in American political reasoning that relies on unfettered in-
> dividualism.[25]

NONPARTISANSHIP UNDER ATTACK

The question of nonpartisan local elections is "a continuing issue,"
as Arthur Bromage states. "It has been debated and will be argued
for decades." [26] This is particularly true for California at the present time. The increasing partisan competition at the state and
national levels has resulted in an inevitable reëxamination of
politics in city and county.

In part this is the result of specific local conditions, some examples of which are noted below. But more important is the attitude of many Democratic politicians in California that their
party interests would be better served by more active and direct

----

[24] National Municipal League, *A Guide for Charter Commissions,* 3d ed. (1957),
p. 36. The league constructs a straw-man in this official statement. Regardless of
other merits or demerits of the partisan election, there is little evidence that
partisan races are decided "solely" on the basis of party considerations. Modern
research on the multiple causation of voting behavior suggests that the party role,
while it may be dominant at times, is generally one of several factors.

[25] Wood, *Suburbia: Its People and Their Politics* (1958), p. 157.

[26] Bromage, "Partisan Elections in Cities," *National Municipal Review,* XL (May,
1951), 250.

participation in municipal and county elections. This springs from the belief that nonpartisanship has been a "privileged sanctuary" from which Republicans have derived partisan advantages. For example, Farrelly and Fox, writing in 1954, state: "It is virtually impossible to build an enduring precinct organization without the foundation of local campaigns. The killing of partisan spirit in municipal elections and the resultant weakening of party machinery means that the Democrats are precluded from mobilizing the vast voting potential found in their registration majority." [27]

The Democratic party has made overwhelming gains in partisan races since 1954 despite the alleged handicap. Nevertheless, Democrats continue to be interested in the formally nonpartisan races. The California Democratic Council Committee on Political Action recommended to the 1957 convention of the council that it "adopt a legislative action program to make county and municipal offices (Judicial and School Board offices excepted) partisan offices." [28] And the election-reform study committee of the 1959 Issues Conference of the same body reported that of the some 300–400 persons on the committee, "there was surprising unanimity that the continuance of non-partisan elections was of immediate concern. There was a very wide agreement that policy-making positions such as members of city councils and county boards of supervisors should be handled on a partisan basis. Reasons presented included the fact that these were offices in which persons were being groomed for partisan office anyway, and that Republican vantage has been cloaked frequently in non-partisanship." However, the study committee noted, "a trial period, in which fresh vigorous leadership in the party proves its trustworthiness may be necessary before the public is easily convinced of its merits [i.e., partisanship at the local level]." [29]

Some of the motivation for the California Democratic Council action in 1959 may have resulted from the knowledge that legislation was pending in Sacramento to make all county and municipal elections partisan. And the approval of the bill AB 1351 by the Assembly Elections Committee on a straight party vote may

---

[27] "Capricious California: A Democratic Dilemma," *Frontier*, VI (November, 1954). See p. 179.
[28] California Democratic Council Convention, *Report* (1957), p. 20.
[29] California Democratic Council, *CDC Issues Conference*, Election Reform Summary Report (March, 1959), pp. 3–4.

be partly explained by the council action. In any event, the bill died on the Assembly floor, and it was clear that the Democratic caucus, for 1959 at least, had been persuaded not to push for its adoption.

Despite the absence of such state legislation, the parties play a role in local politics, to be discussed at greater length in chapter vi. Such activity is not of recent origin. In 1947, for example, the San Francisco Democratic organization was active in behalf of mayoralty candidate and incumbent Congressman Frank Havenner.[30] This was repeated in 1955, when the Democratic County Central Committee officially endorsed another candidate for mayor, which led to a series of critical letters and an editorial in the *San Francisco Chronicle*.[31] To the south, the *Los Angeles Times* in the same year expressed concern over "the intrusion of apparently left-wing controlled Democratic Party influences meddling in practically every traditionally nonpartisan City Council race and the Board of Education contests as well."[32] In 1957, the Los Angeles City Council races were classed as "another of those nonpartisan campaigns with partisan overtones," and the seventh-district contest was characterized as one where the two opposing candidates were running with the full backing and support of the respective party organizations.[33] In 1959, the San Francisco mayoralty contest was between the incumbent, Christopher, a former Republican candidate for the United States Senate, and Wolden, a recently registered Democrat backed officially by a majority of the county Democratic Central Committee.

But it was in Oakland that the strongest example of partisanship could be observed. Here, in the 1959 city-council and school-board elections, the Democratic County Central Committee officially endorsed a slate of Democratic candidates and went on to prepare a "slate mailer" to all registered Democrats in the city urging them to vote for the "officially endorsed Democratic candidates." This marked the first occasion in California in recent years that a central committee had taken an official stand in school elections. Even with respect to the city races, the party activity was unusually vigorous. Oakland, too, is the first Cali-

---

[30] *San Francisco Chronicle*, July 31, 1947.

[31] See, for example, "Partisanship Went Out With Ruef," *San Francisco Chronicle*, November 4, 1955.

[32] "Council Contests in Seven Districts," *Los Angeles Times*, April 3, 1955.

[33] "Elections Stir Los Angeles," *Christian Science Monitor*, May 23, 1957.

fornia city in which a charter amendment to permit partisan elections has been actively discussed, again by the Democratic County Central Committee.

These instances of partisan overtones in nonpartisan local elections are not unique to California, of course. Ignoring such obvious examples as Boston and Chicago, in nonpartisan Denver, for example, "whether coincidentally or not, the finalists each four years are always, respectively, a Democrat and a Republican." [34] In Seattle's nonpartisan mayoralty race in 1955, "partisan politics played a part. . . . The election result is interpreted as an indication that the G.O.P. organization here is in good shape." [35] In Salt Lake City in 1959, "another former Republican governor, J. Bracken Lee of Utah, an ultraconservative now calling himself an independent, is in a hot clash with Democratic state senator Bruce S. Jenkins for the technically nonpartisan office of mayor." [36] Traditionally, party leaders look to local election results as a key to partisan trends. The party most successful at the local level across the nation typically contends that "the elections clearly indicate a swing to our party," while the losers claim that "local issues featured the election, and there is no connection with national party fortunes."

In other states, too, a return to the partisan ballot is being promoted. In 1958, Cleveland voters amended the city charter, changing the method of nominating the mayor from a nonpartisan basis to a partisan primary.[37] Also in Cleveland, the Study Group on Metropolitan Organization recommended that the members of the proposed metropolitan council and the metropolitan executive should be nominated by a partisan primary before a general election.[38] Ludwig reports a movement in Minnesota to place

---

[34] "Denver Race Heads for Tossup Climax," *Christian Science Monitor*, June 15, 1959.

[35] "Seattle Sees Good Government," *Christian Science Monitor*, March 17, 1956.

[36] "Election Battles Around the U.S.," *San Francisco Chronicle*, November 2, 1959.

[37] *National Municipal Review*, XLVII (July, 1958), 340.

[38] The committee reasoned: "Some unifying forces are needed in the metropolitan community to integrate the wide-ranging interest groups and to establish the basic lines of political argument for the voters who must make the ultimate decisions. The two-party system has proven to be the best agent for this purpose . . . . Additionally, the prospect of competition for a political position of the importance of the chief executive of the metropolitan government can serve to stimulate the energy and community consciousness of the two political parties." *Government Organization for Metropolitan Cleveland* (Report to the Cleveland Metropolitan Services Commission, 1959), pp. 7–9.

party labels on the local ballot,[39] while in St. Louis the Board of Freeholders' proposed metropolitan charter provided for partisan elections, in direct contrast to the recommendations of the metropolitan survey team.[40]

None of this should be taken as evidence of a trend, either in California or in the nation, toward increased partisanship in local affairs. Unfortunately, the facts are too scanty to provide a clear perspective of the direction and intensity of the conflicting partisan-nonpartisan currents. The examples indicate, however, the continued introduction of partisan considerations into legally nonpartisan elections. They reveal, also, a questioning of the basic theoretical underpinnings of nonpartisanship and a refusal to accept without challenge the principles espoused by its advocates.

This is as it should be. The democratic process demands that we continuously examine our political institutions and strive to make them more fit to meet the current needs of a free society. The genius of the American people has been this ability to adjust pragmatically the fabric of their political system without doing violence to basic democratic principles.

To be effective, this kind of continuing reëvaluation of our political institutions must be based on an understanding of the facts as they really are and not as we might wish them to be. This is the thesis underlying the remaining chapters of this book.

---

[39] Ludwig, "No Place for Parties," *National Civic Review*, XLVIII (May, 1959), 237.

[40] Metropolitan Board of Freeholders, St. Louis-St. Louis County, Mo., *Proposed Plan of the Greater St. Louis City-County District* (1959); Metropolitan St. Louis Survey, *Path of Progress for Metropolitan St. Louis* (1957), pp. 79–80.

4

The Study: Field Work and Questionnaire

TWO MAJOR TYPES OF SOCIAL SCIENCE INVESTIGATION are described in *Research Methods in the Behavioral Sciences:* the exploratory and the hypothesis testing. The first attempts to discover what *is* rather than to predict what will be found. From its findings may come knowledge about important relationships between variables, but more definite proof of these relationships must await hypothesis testing. The description continues, pointing out that hypothesis testing is ideally more suited to laboratory experimentation, exploratory discovery to the field study. While it need not be confined wholly to exploratory procedures,

> the great strength of the field type of study is its inductive procedure, its potentiality for discovering significant variables and basic relations that would never be found if we were confined to research dictated by a hypothetical-deductive model. Thus, the field study and the survey are the great protection in social science against the sterility and triviality of premature model building.[1]

If sound model building is, indeed, based on an adequate body of factual data, it is clear that such is lacking in a study of local politics in the United States and, more particularly, California. The scholarly journals and books are largely devoid of recent discussions of the subject and the popular magazines and newspapers rarely treat the question with objectivity and analytical skill. Of necessity, then, this is largely an exploratory study.

The Six-City Study.—A large share of the findings and conclusions reported in the pages to follow derive from information gathered in six California cities in 1955. Early in the formative stages of the project, the decision was reached that it would be more desirable to attempt several short investigations rather than to concentrate on but one community. Such a study would permit comparisons and provide a broader, although admittedly "thinner," set of facts on which to base generalizations.[2]

---

[1] Katz, "Field Studies," *in* Festinger and Katz, eds., *Research Methods in the Behavioral Sciences* (1953), p. 75.

A specific and outstanding example of the field study is found in *Southern Politics*. Key indicates (p. vi) the thinking which prompted the choice of this approach: "It was realized that no matter how complete the collection of legal, statistical, and other documentary data, there could be no genuine understanding of the electoral process without intimate acquaintance with the day to day practice of politics; consequently it was planned from the beginning to engage in extensive field interviewing. It was thought that the raw material for interpreting the political process could best be obtained from those active in public life. . . . The persons whose testimony was sought were in large measure active or retired politicians. . . . A large number of other persons, participants in the political scene or close observers . . . publishers, editors, newspaper reporters, leaders in labor and industry and farm organizations . . . leading spirits in reform movements, and students of government and politics."

[2] That the writer is aware of the limitations of the one-man (and wife) short-term field trip may be made clear by citing two recent community studies, both of which stand as landmarks in the attention paid to local politics: In the first, two scholars spent three years observing the daily life of a community of 3,000 persons in upper New York State: Vidich and Bensman, *Small Town in Mass Society* (1958). In the second, a small army of professors and graduate students spent months examining in detail the political and administrative life of an English town of 20,000: Birch, *Small-Town Politics* (1959).

To permit meaningful comparison as well as to avoid the pitfalls of the more intricate and complex large city (a serious problem given the limitations of time and resources), none of the six had a population larger than 150,000. While it was not deemed possible to arrive at a "cross section," the selected cities did represent as many different aspects of the state's urban life as feasible.

A brief description of each of the six cities is included in the appendix. Suffice it to say here that the cities—Berkeley, Chico, Fresno, Maywood, Pomona, and San Leandro—included communities ranging in population at the time of the study from 13,000 to 118,000; four cities used the council-manager, one the mayor-council and one the commission form of government (now abandoned). Four are situated in metropolitan centers and two in rural areas; four are racially homogeneous and two racially and ethnically mixed; each has varying degrees and types of local industry and commercial development; one city is in the Sacramento Valley, one in the San Joaquin Valley, two in the Los Angeles metropolitan area and two in the San Francisco Bay region; three are relatively stable in terms of physical and population growth and three are rapidly expanding. The location of these six cities is indicated on the following map.

In each city initial interviews were held with all elective and key administrative personnel in the city government, newspapermen, and political party officials. From this standard base group, suggestions came as to others in the community who had special knowledge of the local political situation. These generally included business and labor officials, ministers, and women's-club leaders. An attempt was made to interview respondents with a variety of experience and background in terms of occupation, place of residence, sympathy with the incumbent city administration and political affiliation. Other than this, however, no attempt was made to interview a "sample" of the community's population. All interviews were "off the record." While a carefully prepared series of questions was generally used, it was often more beneficial to allow the respondent to "ramble and reminisce" rather than to attempt exactly to follow the schedule. With hardly any exceptions, the more than 100 persons interviewed were most willing to participate. In fact, many seemed to welcome the opportunity to "unload" to a disinterested stranger with no local ax to grind, and the frankness of many was at times surprising.

In every city, local voting and registration data were gathered from official city and county records; and economic and demo-

The six California cities
in which local politics were
studied (with 1960 population)

CHICO (15,000)

BERKELEY (110,000)

SAN LEANDRO (66,000)

FRESNO (133,000)

POMONA (67,000)

MAYWOOD (15,000)

graphic data from planning departments and chambers of commerce. Newspaper files were examined, particularly for the period around recent elections. Preliminary reports for each city were prepared and sent to qualified observers of the local scene for comments and suggestions.[3]

The Questionnaire.—To complement the six-cities' findings, a questionnaire was mailed in 1955 to community leaders throughout the state requesting their views on a variety of matters concerning local politics. These leaders—totaling 718—chosen because of their identifiability and accessibility, included mayors, city managers, daily-newspaper editors or publishers, and the county central-committee chairman of each political party. The League of California Cities, state officials of both political parties, and the California Newspaper Publishers' Association coöperated. Copies of the questionnaires (one for mayors, managers, and newspapermen, the other for county party chairmen) are included in the appendix.

Of the distributed questionnaires 320, or 45 per cent were returned. With the exception of the very small cities of the state, the returns were quite representative, both in terms of population and form of government.[4] The number included 32 per cent of the mayors, 38 per cent of the editors or publishers, 50 per cent of the county-committee chairmen, and 53 per cent of the city managers or other local administrative officials in the state. At least one reply was received from 192 (61 per cent) of the state's 315 cities, including 139 (75 per cent) of the 185 cities with a population of more than 5,000. Similarly, replies were received

---

[3] A detailed account of the political scene in the six cities is contained in the writer's doctoral dissertation. "The Politics of Nonpartisan Elections in California Cities" (1957), which includes the separate city reports as appendices.

[4] Distributed according to population, the cities replying to the questionnaire were as follows:

DISTRIBUTION AND RETURN OF CITY QUESTIONNAIRES,
BY SIZE OF CITY

| Size of city | Number of cities: | | Per cent replied |
	In state	Replied	
Less than 10,000	183	90	49
10,000 to 50,000	104	82	79
50,000 to 100,000	17	13	76
100,000 and more	11	7	64
TOTAL	315	192	61

from 58 (50 per cent) of the county central-committee chairmen (28 Republicans and 30 Democrats) from 44 (76 per cent) of the state's 58 counties. A "composite" reply was developed for each city from which more than one response had been returned, and the replies were coded and prepared for machine tabulation. Comments by respondents also were analyzed and summarized.

A Reminder.—No one can be more conscious than the political reporter of the subjectivity of many of his own impressions; besides, the analyst becomes quickly aware that many community "experts" simply do not know the facts. More than once in the course of this study, a qualified respondent, either in the interviewing process or in the written questionnaire, revealed that his impressions were at variance with reality or that his knowledge of some basic point was deficient.

More difficult to evaluate are the situations where the respondent may know the facts but either refuses to divulge them or, worse yet, concocts a statement to his liking. This is more likely to happen in a written questionnaire than in an interview where inconsistencies and incorrect statements may be followed up by the interviewer.

To say this does not, of course, damn the field-study approach or the findings reported below. The fact that a study is based, in

By form of government, the sample was distributed in this manner:

DISTRIBUTION AND RETURN OF CITY QUESTIONNAIRES,
BY FORM OF GOVERNMENT

	Number of cities:		
Form of government	In state	Replied	Per cent replied
Council-manager	117	100	85
Appointed mayor	100	85	85
Elected mayor	17	15	88
Appointed mayor-council	190	87	46
Cities less than 5,000	129	51	40
Cities more than 5,000	61	36	59
Elected mayor-council	7	4	57
Commission, elected mayor	1	1	100
TOTAL	315	192	61

In Appendix B, tables are included showing the distribution of the replies according to the type of respondent and, for the county-chairman questionnaire, according to county population and the chairman's party affiliation.

part, on subjective data does not rule out its validity or value: "The notion of the subjective is [often] confused immediately with the notion of unreliability. . . . Whether subjective reports are necessarily unreliable, invalid, and untranslated into behavior is a matter for empirical study, not for preconceptions." [5] Social science would be handicapped indeed if attitudes, impressions, and opinions were ruled out. It must be remembered, too, that the existence of a subjective attitude or opinion, even when not in accord with the truth, is itself an objective fact and frequently one of importance. Who people *think* are community leaders is significant in the determination of who actually *are* community leaders.

One more serious problem remains, however. This is a study of nonpartisan elections, but the problem of isolating the specific factor of nonpartisanship is almost insoluble. Theoretically, a historical examination might be undertaken of elections immediately before and after the introduction of the nonpartisan ballot and the differences and similarities noted. But no such examination (even if data were available) could isolate the feature of the nonpartisan ballot from the forces which had resulted in its adoption in the first place. Schulz indicates this in suggesting that, "independent voting in western communities probably is the cause rather than the effect of the adoption of nonpartisan devices." [6] Stone, Price, and Stone echo this problem of separating cause from effect: "This study has been unable to make metaphysical distinctions between the effect of the new form of government [the council-manager plan] and the effect of the motives of its advocates and supporters." [7] As for nonpartisanship, the fact that the shift in ballot form has generally been accompanied in its adoption by a host of other changes—the council-manager plan, civil-service reform, and other ballot measures such as the at-large election, to name but a few— complicates the problem even further. Lane Lancaster observes that "it is very hard to appraise the effect of the nonpartisan system, because it is normally only one of the factors which have to be considered in

---

[5] Hyman, "Interviewing as a Scientific Procedure," *in* Lerner and Lasswell, eds., *The Policy Sciences* (1951), p. 207.

[6] Schulz, *American City Government, Its Machinery and Process* (1949), p. 255.

[7] Stone, Price, and Stone, *City Manager Government in the United States* (1940), p. 258.

estimating the effectiveness of the governments which use it." [8]

A more fruitful avenue of appraisal might be to compare the local political process under a partisan electoral system with a similar community operating under the nonpartisan ballot. Here the problem of finding two communities theoretically similar in every respect but the form of ballot would be, of course, the key methodological hurdle. The variety of relevant conditions revealed in the course of this study conducted within a single state graphically illustrate this problem. Nevertheless, such an appraisal would no doubt have promise. In this study, attempts at comparisons are made, but such is the state of the literature that few opportunities exist to do so, even on a highly limited basis.

Finally, certain features of a local nonpartisan election might be compared with related aspects at the state or national level, for example the impact of a run-off election system. Here, of course, the differences in context rule out all but the most carefully developed comparisons, some highly primitive examples of which are indicated below.

This, then, is a study of local elections in a nonpartisan setting. The extent to which it is also a study of a *unique* election system must await the development of more complete comparative data than now exist.

---

[8] Quoted in Mitchell, "Non-Partisan Nominations and Elections," *Public Business,* I: 10 (July, 1953), 4.

THE FINDINGS

5

Mayors, Councilmen, and Elections

THIS STUDY BEGINS WITH THE END OF THE ELECTION PROC-
ess, the successful candidate. Over the centuries, political
science has concerned itself with the characteristics of such formally designated leaders of a society. Although in a city, perhaps
even more than in a state or nation, the real locus of civic leadership may not always be found in the roster of public officials, the
elected representatives of the city will have a great influence on
the character and quality of municipal government and administration. Also, the "product" of the election, the elected councilman or mayor, provides a convenient introduction to various aspects of the political process itself. The elected representative re-

flects, to some degree, the pattern of groups and interests in the political life of the community and, in a sense, the characteristics and attitudes of its citizenry.

A "COMPOSITE" COUNCILMAN

The data, based on the 38 incumbents in office in the six cities at the time of the study, may be summarized by describing a "composite" councilman, that is, by attributing to a hypothetical individual the characteristics most frequently encountered in the group as a whole. The necessary qualifications and exceptions to such generalization are to be found in the pages to follow.

The "California Councilman" is a man of 45 to 50 years of age, engaged in some professional, managerial, or sales activity and living in the "better" part of town. He belongs to a service club, is probably a Mason, a member of a veterans group and of the chamber of commerce. He is a Protestant but not necessarily affiliated with any church. He had no previous official city experience, although he was active in Community Chest, Red Cross, or related activities. He is a registered Republican, but has not taken a very extensive part in partisan politics. He has lived in the city for a considerable length of time.[1]

Age and Length of City Residence.—The incumbent mayors and councilmen in the six cities fell into the categories shown in table 5:

---

[1] This description is remarkably similar to one based on a study of 283 councilmen and mayors serving in Los Angeles County in 1957: "The 'average' city councilman in one of the fifty-three cities which existed in Los Angeles County on June 1, 1957, is likely to have the following characteristics: He is male, about forty-eight years old, and the chances are three to one that he was not born in California. However, despite the fact that he came from out of the state, the odds are greatly in favor of his having lived in his community for more than ten years, and there is more than a fifty-fifty chance that he is a relative newcomer to his job, having held office for four years or less. To state what his business interests are is a little more difficult. If he has had professional training, it is likely to have been in law, engineering, or science, and if he is a nonprofessional, he probably owns his own commercial business. There is even a fair chance that he is retired. His party affiliation is more definite; the odds are two to one that he is a registered Republican." Huckshorn, "Spotlight on City Councilmen," *BGR Observer* (November, 1957), p. 1. This study is cited throughout this chapter without further reference.

TABLE 5

AGE AND LENGTH OF RESIDENCE OF MAYORS AND COUNCILMEN

Age of officials		Residence of officials	
Years	Number	Years	Number
30-39	7	0-9	4
40-49	12	10-19	8
50-59	9	20-29	6
60-69	7	30-39	6
70 and older	1	40-49	11
		50 and more	1
Not available	2	Not available	2
Average: 49		Average: 28	

Distributed by city, the pattern emerges from table 6.

TABLE 6

AVERAGE AGE AND LENGTH OF RESIDENCE
OF MAYORS AND COUNCILMEN

City	Average age	Average years of city residence
Chico	41	34
Fresno	52	42
Pomona	44	23
Maywood	53	22
San Leandro	49	16
Berkeley	52	26

Significant variations between the six councils are apparent. Chico, for example, had "young" councilmen with an average age of 41, while in Maywood, the average age was 53. The differences bore no relationship to the median age of the total city population as reported in the 1950 census, which varied only from 31 to 34 in the six cities.

The average length of city residence is remarkable, considering the extent to which California cities are composed of newcomers. Elected officials are clearly less mobile than the population generally. Six of the thirty-six incumbents for whom information was available had been born in the city which they now served, another seven had moved into the community before

reaching age twenty, and thirteen had come to the city during
their twenties. Only ten, 28 per cent, had not lived in the city
before World War II, while the state's population had increased
by almost 100 per cent between 1940 and 1955.

As indicated in the table, however, the impact of these facts is
felt more heavily by some communities than others. The two cities
with the longest average length of city residence (and containing
five of the six "native sons") were Chico and Fresno. These are
both farm centers, relatively isolated from contact with other
communities, whereas the other four cities are in the midst of
either the Los Angeles or the San Francisco-Oakland metropolitan complex. In contrast, San Leandro, the most rapidly expanding of the six cities, was the lowest in terms of length of residence,
and two-thirds of the council were postwar arrivals.

The six-city record is borne out by the Los Angeles survey.
The average age of the councilmen in that county was 49, identical with the six-city figure. Councilmen in southern California
are slightly more mobile than in the smaller all-state sample, but
the tendency toward long residence is still pronounced. Fewer
than 20 per cent of the councilmen in Los Angeles County had
lived in the city in which they held office for less than ten years,
while almost 30 per cent were residents for thirty years or more.

Sex.—Only three members (eight per cent) of the councils
were women. In Fresno the incumbent was the first of her sex
ever to serve on the city commission; in Chico no woman had
served for more than thirty years. Of the six cities, only Berkeley
has had a tradition of regular service of women. At times, there
have been as many as three women on the council, but from 1947
to 1958, no more than one woman had served at any given time.
A second woman was elected in 1959. In the Los Angeles County
study, the proportion of women was even smaller, 18 out of 283,
only 6 per cent.

This record is less a result of the failure of women to win votes
than it is their reluctance to stand for office. In the six cities in
1954–1955, for example, 59 men ran for the office of councilman
or mayor as compared with eight women, only 12 per cent of the
total; and four of the eight were candidates in the unusually large
field in the Fresno elections of that year. Of the eight, three were
elected.

Occupation.[2]—Using the United States Census' definitions for purposes of classification, the 38 elected mayors and councilmen in the six cities were members (five of them retired) of the following occupational groups:

> Thirteen were "professional, technical and kindred workers": 4—teachers or educators, 3—engineers, 2—attorneys, 2 accountants, 1—pharmacist, 1—funeral director.
>
> Twelve were "managers, officials, and proprietors, except farm": 5—merchants, 2—service-station proprietors, 2—union officials, 2—manufacturing-or service-plant executives, 1—restaurant owner.
>
> Eight were "sales workers": 5—insurance or real-estate agents, 3—representatives for manufacturing firms.
>
> Two were "housewives."
>
> Two were "craftsmen": one contractor and one mechanic.
>
> One was a farmer, also in the real estate business.

No councilmen in any of the six cities came from the following classes of occupations: "clerical and kindred workers," "operatives and kindred workers," "private household workers," "service workers, except private household," "farm laborers and foremen," and "laborers, except farm and mine."

The Los Angeles County survey indicated much the same pattern. Of the 283 councilmen, 81 were professional men, 95 businessmen, 43 salesmen, 12 agriculturists, 9 housewives, and the remainder white-collar workers and retired persons. Huckshorn concludes that "labor in relation to its populational strength is tremendously under-represented on the city councils, while businessmen are represented out of proportion to their actual number in the populace. . . . Councilmen who own a commercial business or manufacturing concern or who are business executives constitute nearly one-third of all individuals serving on the fifty-three city councils. . . . Only a little over 4 per cent of the council-

---

[2] Occupational data for former city officials in the six cities and for officials in other cities were obtained from the affidavits of registration, which every registered voter in California must sign. However, these proved to be faulty, because they indicate the occupation as of the time of registration and are not necessarily current. Therefore, this summary treats only those few councilmen and mayors who were in office at the time of the study and whose occupation could be checked independently. The sample appears representative of the occupational status of mayors and councilmen, generally, and the findings are supported by the Los Angeles study.

men would, by reason of their vocation, represent the multitude of skilled or unskilled workers." [3]

Place of Residence.—In Chico, Fresno, Pomona, and Berkeley, elected officials and advisory board members appointed by the council tended to reside in the more well-to-do sections of the community and, at times, within particular neighborhoods. For example, in Fresno, all seven commissioners resided within a few blocks of each other in the northwest area of the city, the location of the more expensive homes. In Berkeley, only five of the 42 incumbent councilmen and advisory board members had their homes in the south and west sections of the city, an area including about 50 per cent of the city's residents and featured by relatively less expensive homes. The remaining 37 officials lived in the more well-to-do hill neighborhoods. In Maywood, the city was too small for such geographical concentration. In San Leandro the distribution was more representative geographically of the city as a whole. The existence of district plans of council representation in both San Leandro and Pomona forced a certain amount of geographical dispersion.

Community Affiliations: Religious, Service, and Social.—The frequency with which the mayors and councilmen belonged to lodges and service clubs may be summarized as follows:

At least 25 of the men belonged to one or more service clubs, such as Kiwanis, Rotary, Lions or Optimist. Each of the three women was a member of one or more organizations such as the Business and Professional Women's Club, the American Association for University Women or the League of Women Voters.

Most of the officials had participated in some sort of community activity, such as community chest, Red Cross or YMCA fund raising. At least nine of the men had been active in the local chamber of commerce, while ten had served on some official city board or commission prior to their appointment or election to the city council.

At least thirteen of the men belonged to lodges other than Masonic, such as the Moose or Elks. Fifteen belonged to some Masonic order, and at least seven of the men were members of the local American Legion and/or Veterans of Foreign Wars post.

---

[3] Huckshorn, *op. cit.*, p. 3.

All but four indicated they were Protestants (including Latter Day Saints and Christian Scientists), although several said they were not affiliated with any church. Three were Roman Catholics, and one was of Jewish parentage but unaffiliated himself.

No data are available by which this small sample might be compared with the population of the six cities, but it would appear that local officials are considerably more active in the types of organizations described above, with the possible exception of churches, than the citizens generally.

Partisan Affiliation.—Local officials in the six cities were predominantly registered Republicans, as table 7 (considering only those registered with the two major parties) indicates.

TABLE 7

MAYORS AND COUNCILMEN, REGISTERED REPUBLICAN

City	Per cent of voters registered Republicans 1955	Mayors and councilmen: 1931-1955			Advisory board members: 1955		
		Republicans	Total	Per cent Republicans	Republicans	Total	Per cent Republicans
Chico	50	14	23	61	22	28	79
Fresno	33	10	20	50	19	47	40
Pomona	50	22	26	85	18	22	82
Maywood	31	11	21	52	4	8	50
San Leandro	39	17	23	74	15	24	63
Berkeley	48	25	30	83	28	33	85
TOTAL	42	99	143	69	106	162	65

NOTE: Councilmen include those in office in each city during approximately the past 22 to 25 years; identical information could not be obtained for each city.

The data also reveal that although almost as many Democrats as Republicans competed for office in the six cities, Republicans had a better record at the polls in every city. As table 8 indicates, although only 52 per cent of the candidates were Republicans, 70 per cent of those elected were from that party.

No data concerning other personal characteristics could be readily obtained from a larger number of cities, but a broader survey of the partisan affiliation of California local officials was possible. With these data, the oft-stated but never documented assertion could be tested that the ranks of California's local office holders are dominated by registered Republicans. The party affiliation of 2,895 local officials was determined, including, with very few exceptions, every mayor, city councilman, county supervisor, city manager, city clerk, city attorney, city assessor (where a separate official), county clerk, district attorney, sheriff, county assessor and (where such an officer exists) county administrative officer in California in 1955.[4]

TABLE 8

CANDIDATES AND WINNERS FOR CITY OFFICE, BY PARTY

	Republicans			Democrats		
		Winners			Winners	
City	Candi-dates	Num-ber	Per cent	Candi-dates	Num-ber	Per cent
Chico (1945-1955)	18	11	61	9	5	56
Fresno (1945-1955)	27	10	37	27	6	22
Pomona (1947-1955)	41	14	34	31	2	6
Maywood (1946-1954)	13	4	31	32	9	28
San Leandro (1946-1954)	13	8	62	20	4	20
Berkeley (1947-1955)	38	20	53	21	3	14
TOTAL	150	67	45	140	29	21

The data indicate that the persons holding important elective and appointive office in California's cities and counties tend to be Republicans by a three to two margin, almost the direct reverse of the distribution of the state's registered voters. The Los Angeles study revealed the identical pattern with two-thirds of all councilmen registered Republican. The party affiliation of the various local office holders throughout California is set forth in table 9.

The evidence indicates that the Republican majority is even more pronounced in the larger cities and counties of the state. For example, in the 26 cities of more than 50,000, 80 per cent of the mayors and 68 per cent of the city councilmen were registered

---

[4] In approximately twenty counties, including Los Angeles with its 46 cities, the registration data were collected personally by direct tabulation from the individual affidavits of registration on file in each county court house. In the remaining counties, a canvas by mail was attempted. Using the *State Roster of Public Officials* as a source, lists of the names of local officials were mailed to the various county clerks with a request that they indicate the party affiliation of the person. A covering letter indicated the purpose of the study. Replies were received from every county. By inadvertence, only the town of Plymouth (1950 population: 382) is missing of the state's 315 cities as of 1955.

TABLE 9

CALIFORNIA LOCAL OFFICIALS BY PARTY REGISTRATION, 1955

Official	Republicans		Democrats	
	Number	Per cent	Number	Per cent
Mayor	181	60	119	40
City councilman	768	58	545	42
County supervisor	153	54	128	46
District attorney	30	52	28	48
Sheriff	25	46	31	54
County clerk	37	64	21	36
County assessor	35	63	21	37
County administrative officer	5	45	6	55
City manager	74	66	38	34
City attorney	164	61	107	39
City clerk	191	64	107	36
City assessor	24	62	15	38
TOTAL	1,687	59	1,166	41

NOTE: The data exclude 42 unaffiliated local officials.

Republicans, a substantially higher percentage than for the state as a whole.[5] Only Los Angeles, San Francisco, San Bernardino, and South Gate of these larger cities had a majority of Democratic councilmen. The difference when related to population was not significant for county supervisors; 51 per cent of the supervisors in the twelve counties of a population exceeding 250,000 were registered Republican as compared with 54 per cent for the state as a whole. However, a substantially higher percentage of administrative officers were registered Republican in these larger counties than in the state generally—64 per cent of the sheriffs, 67 per cent of the district attorneys, 82 per cent of the assessors and 67 per cent of the clerks.

Of the state's 25 separately elected mayors in 1955, 19 (76 per cent) were Republicans. Of the twelve elective mayor cities with

[5] The extent to which the nonpartisan ballot is a factor in this Republican predominance of local officialdom cannot be determined on the basis of a study of one state, of course, and no national survey of the partisan affiliation of local officials has ever been undertaken. However, the California figures do contrast with those from two states with partisan local elections. Following the 1959 local elections, *The Christian Science Monitor* reported that in New York State there were twenty-eight Democratic mayors to the G.O.P.'s twenty-five. In Indiana, the state's ten largest cities "went to the Democrats," and the article reported that in 1955, the Democrats took 72 out of 106 contests for mayor (November 5 and 6, 1959).

a population of more than 50,000, eleven (92 per cent) had Republican chief executives.

The data were examined to ascertain whether relatively more Republican mayors, councilmen, and supervisors were elected to local office in counties with a relatively heavy Republican registration. Only the slightest evidence of such a relationship is apparent, far below the level of significance. Data are not available to make a similar comparison with all cities of the state. However, the cities of Los Angeles County were examined. Table 10 indicates clearly that the more heavily registered Republican the city, the more often its elected mayor and councilmen tend to be members of the G.O.P.

TABLE 10

City-Wide Republican Registration and Republican Representation
on City Councils in Los Angeles County, 1955
(Including Mayors)

Republican per cent of total registration in city	Number of cities	Proportion of city council members registered Republican					
		None	1/5	2/5	3/5	4/5	All
0-29	0	0	0	0	0	0	0
30-39	17	1	2	8	4	2	0
40-49	8	0	0	0	4	2	2
50-59	9	0	0	1	2	3	3
60-69	8	0	0	0	1	2	5
70-100	3	0	0	0	0	0	3
TOTAL	45	1	2	9	11	9	13

NOTE: Most cities have five-man councils, including the mayor. Cities with six-, seven-, nine-, or fifteen-member councils were classed according to the nearest fraction. One additional city council was evenly divided between the two parties, resulting from a vacancy.

Republicans are often elected in Democratic cities, but Democrats are not as likely to be so favored in communities with a Republican majority. Fourteen of the 25 cities in which the Republicans were the minority party in terms of registered voters had a majority of councilmen registered Republican. Of the 20 cities with a Republican majority among the electorate, however, only one had a city council with a majority of Democratic members. In 13 cities in Los Angeles County, all councilmen were Republicans, but in only one city none were.

Nonpartisan Voting and Partisan Trends.—The period from 1955 to 1959 witnessed a dramatic shift in California partisan offices, with Democrats increasing their proportion of state and national legislative seats from 39 per cent to 60 per cent. It is clear, also, that during this period there was considerable discussion, primarily by Democrats, about the desirability of party participation in nonpartisan elections. It is not possible readily to assess the degree to which this took place. Nevertheless, a study is feasible to determine the extent to which, if at all, nonpartisan elections followed partisan voting trends. Did the proportion of Democratic local office holders increase during a period when the state's voters were returning more Democrats to state and national office?

Table 11, based on data from the twelve largest counties including approximately 80 per cent of the state's population, indicates that the answer to this question is a qualified yes.

While the proportion of registered Democrats holding local office increased 5 per cent, a significant shift took place in Alameda County only. In the 26 large cities of the state referred to above, Republicans still dominated the ranks of mayors and councilmen to a greater degree than was true of city officials in the twelve largest counties generally. In 1959, Republicans still held twenty of the mayoralty seats in these cities, a decline of only one seat, and 62 per cent of the councilman posts, a decline from the 68 per cent figure noted above.

The increase of 5 per cent in Democratic local office holders during a period when that party's percentage of the two-party registration in the state increased by only 1.6 per cent is noteworthy. However, it is impossible to say whether this shift is a trend or a temporary deviation, or, in fact, has any relationship to partisan voting behavior.

SOME CHARACTERISTICS OF THE ELECTION
OF LOCAL OFFICIALS

The Number of Candidates and Intensity of Competition.—In the six cities, public officials have generally faced competition in local

TABLE 11

Mayors and Councilmen by Party Registration
(Twelve Largest Counties, 1955-1959)

County	Number of mayors and councilmen						Change for Democrats	
	1955			1959				
	Republicans	Democrats	Unaffiliated	Republicans	Democrats	Unaffiliated	Number	Per cent
Alameda	41	17	2	29	30	1	+13	+22
Contra Costa	29	29	0	27	31	0	+2	+3
Fresno	28	45	0	28	44	1	−1	−2
Kern	18	19	2	13	23	0	+4	+13
Los Angeles	161	78	1	160	87	4	+9	+2
Orange	53	19	0	44	24	0	+5	+9
Sacramento	16	11	0	13	15	1	+4	+11
San Bernardino	24	27	0	28	23	0	−4	−8
San Diego	31	15	0	30	17	0	+2	+3
San Francisco	6	6	0	6	6	0	0	0
San Mateo	39	25	2	41	25	1	0	0
Santa Clara	53	23	1	47	28	2	+5	+6
TOTAL	499	314	8	466	353	10	+39	—
Per cent	61	38	1	56	43	1	—	5

NOTE: The data are based only on cities in existence in 1955. The partisan division is almost identical with this pattern if officials from newly incorporated cities are included.

elections.[6] In only eight races in 75 elections during the 25-year period 1930–1955 was competition absent. Two to four candidates were almost always available for every council or mayor's seat to be filled. Based on this record, there are proportionately fewer uncontested races than is generally true for California state legislative contests. In the 1954 election, for example, 15 of the 80 Assembly seats were uncontested in the primary election, that is, one candidate stood unopposed for both party nominations under the cross-filing law. Fourteen were uncontested in the primary in 1956, and eleven in 1958. Additional seats were uncontested in the general election as a result of successful cross-filing—five in 1958, for example.

Intensity of election competition was measured in this study by the percentage difference in total vote cast between the lowest winning and the highest losing candidate. In each city were examples of close elections in which the margin of victory ranged

---

[6] The several election systems employed in the six cities had the following characteristics. In Maywood and Chico the system is the same, although the former is governed under state law, the latter a charter community. Alternate groups of two or three councilmen stand every two years for four-year terms. Candidates race against the entire field, and the citizen may vote for as many candidates as there are seats to be filled. Plurality victories are permitted. The mayor is selected by the council from among their own members.

This is the system employed in Berkeley, except that the councilmen number eight instead of five, and a separately elected mayor is provided who also serves a four-year term.

San Leandro employed the Maywood-Chico system until 1954. For that election and those to follow, the city was divided into six districts, and a seventh seat was retained at large. Candidates, except for those choosing to run for the at-large seat, must reside in the district for whose seat they wish to run. All seats are elected at large, however. Three district seats are contested every two years, and all terms are for four years. Plurality victories are permitted.

This is the system used in Pomona, with the exception that the at-large seat in that city is filled by a separately elected mayor whose term is for two years. Pomona's council numbers five as contrasted with San Leandro's seven. Runoff elections are required in Pomona for any contest in which a majority is not obtained in the primary.

The Fresno system, now abandoned along with the commission form of government, was extraordinarily and unnecessarily complicated. Three administrative commissionerships, including the mayor, appeared on the ballot every four years. Three separate races were conducted—candidates filing for one or another post as they wished and were qualified. (The public-works post required engineering experience, for example.) Two years later and also for four-year terms, elections were held for four legislative commissionerships. These posts were numbered but with no reference to geographical areas of the city. Candidates filed for one particular numbered seat, although qualifications for all posts were identical. The voter, for this reason, had to keep four separate combinations of opposing candidates in mind. All elections were at large, and plurality victories were permitted.

as low as 1 or 2 per cent. In each city, too, were examples of land-slide victories, where it was evident that the winning candidates had faced little effective competition. At times, the winner's margin of victory was as high as 35–40 per cent over his nearest opponent. The frequency with which close contests occurred is suggested by table 12.

TABLE 12

NUMBER OF ELECTION CONTESTS ACCORDING TO INTENSITY
OF COMPETITION: 1946-1955

City	Margin of difference between lowest winning and highest losing candidate in per cent of the total vote cast				
	0-5	6-10	11-15	16-20	More than 20
Chico	1	0	1	0	2
Fresno	2	0	2	4	7
Pomona	*3*	*4*	*2*	3	4
Maywood	1	1	2	1	0
San Leandro	3	3	1	0	1
Berkeley	3	1	0	1	1

NOTE: This table comprises a variety of election systems, including those where each candidate runs against the field, as contrasted with systems where the total field is divided into several district races. In Pomona, all races indicated by italics were runoff elections. The table excludes uncontested elections. In Berkeley, not all races were included because the former use of second-choice ballots renders analysis impossible.

Again, no attempt was made to compare these data in any comprehensive fashion with related statistics concerning, for example, state elections. The difference in the character of the elections and the composition of the electorate would make such an analysis a speculative one. However, a general measure of competition can be obtained by noting the margin of victory of the winning candidate over the nearest competitor, in terms of per cent of the total vote cast, for California Assembly contests in the 1958 general election. The results appear on the opposite page.[7]

If a 10 per cent margin of victory be classed as the outside limit of a "close" race, then only 31 per cent of the contested 1958 assembly elections can be so described. More than half of the contested winners had victory margins of more than 20 per cent. Of

---

[7] The data on which this analysis is based appear in Greenfield *et al.*, *Legislative Reapportionment: California in National Perspective* (1959), pp. 89–93.

MARGIN OF VICTORY IN ASSEMBLY ELECTIONS, 1958

Percentage of victory	Number of elections
0–5	14
6–10	6
11–15	9
16–20	2
More than 20	33
Unopposed	16
Total	80

the thirty Congressional races in 1958, five were uncontested in the general election. Of the remainder only six fell within a 10 per cent margin of victory, and ten exceeded 20 per cent. Despite difficulties of comparison, it is clear that city races are as frequently and closely competitive as those at higher levels.

Plurality Victories.—One important, but seldom studied, aspect of the local election process is the frequency of plurality victories.

TABLE 13

CANDIDATES WINNING LOCAL ELECTIONS BY A PLURALITY: 1946-1955

City	Number of winning candidates			Lowest winning per cent of total vote cast
	Total	Winning by plurality		
		Number	Per cent	
Chico	11	4	36	37
Fresno	7	5	71	26
Maywood	13	6	46	34
San Leandro	13	9	69	38
Berkeley (1951-1955)	13	5	38	45
TOTAL	57	29	51	—

NOTE: Only contests in which more than two candidates competed are included in the computation. The sample for Berkeley is smaller because the former second-choice balloting makes analysis impossible.

Only a few California cities allow runoff elections. Of the six cities, only Pomona required a second election when candidates failed to obtain a majority in the primary race. The frequency of plurality victories in the remaining five cities is shown in table 13.

In at least one-third of the contests in each of the five cities, winning candidates failed to receive a majority vote. Taking the five cities as a whole, more than half of the winning candidates in contested races received only a plurality vote, and at times the winning vote was as low as 26 per cent of the total vote cast.[8]

The implications of the plurality system are highlighted by the Pomona experience. In that city, in 29 (81 per cent) of the 36 contested races in twenty-five years, no candidate received a majority in the primary election. In 9 (31 per cent) of the ensuing 29 runoff elections, the leader in the primary election was *defeated*. Under the single-election system prevailing in the other five cities, the primary leader would have been declared elected. The Pomona data also indicated that voter participation in runoff elections was 6 to 15 per cent higher than in the primary elections and that runoff elections tended to be much closer than those in which the winner was selected in the primary contest.

More analysis is required in other cities in which runoff elections are required. It is possible, however, that a system requiring the mobilization of a majority of the electorate might necessitate a different pattern of local politics than one in which victory is possible with a lesser vote. Of course, if in a community few candidates compete for local office anyway, the implications of plurality victories are not so significant, because majority elections often result. If, however, there is a tendency for many candidates to stand for a single office, the influence of the electoral system may be profound. A graphic illustration of this was the 1953 Fresno commission race. With a turnout of 59 per cent of those registered to vote, a candidate won with 26 per cent of the total vote cast; in short, 15 per cent of the registered electorate, or an estimated 9 per cent of the adult population, were able to elect a candidate. Such plurality victories complement, even if they do not explain, the informal and unstructured politics which exist in many communities. Individuals and groups may be more likely to enter the political arena if victory is possible without the

---

[8] A facet of multiple-seat elections is "single-shot" voting. In an election to fill four seats, for example, voters vote only for one candidate, on the theory that if they complete their ballot they will, in effect, be taking strength away from their number-one choice. This practice is quite prevalent in the Negro districts in Berkeley, for example, where votes are concentrated behind the Negro candidate, and many voters abstain from voting a full (racially mixed) ticket.

requirement of a majority vote.[9] A potential danger exists, of course, that a council with several members elected by less than a majority will fail to reflect accurately existing community attitudes and expectations and that public confidence in the local legislative body will suffer accordingly.

The Factor of Incumbency.—Under any system of elections, it is claimed that the incumbent has an advantage in election contests. He is generally accorded a preferential place on the ballot, and his name is frequently more familiar to the voter than the

TABLE 14

INCUMBENTS REËLECTED IN CONTESTED ELECTIONS, 1932-1955

	Number		Per cent reëlected
City	Total	Reelected	
Chico	17	12	71
Fresno	25	20	80
Pomona	24	13	54
Maywood	25	15	60
San Leandro	25	14	56
Berkeley	49	43	88
TOTAL	165	117	71

NOTE: The 1954 election in San Leandro was eliminated because the new districting system forced incumbents to compete against each other.

[9] With reference to primary elections at the state level in the South, Key arrives at a contradictory conclusion. There exists, he finds, a relationship between a runoff system and multifactional politics and a contrasting connection between plurality victories and dual factionalism. "The hypothesis runs generally to the effect that with one office to be filled by a plurality vote—that of governor, for example, the organizers of political effort would form alliances in order to maximize their chance of belonging to a combination with a single chance to win. If the man with the largest number of votes takes all, no matter how small a proportion of the total vote they may be, the incentive of political leaders and sub-leaders is to try to maneuver into a winning combination in the first primary. On the other hand, if there is a second voting, a candidate can take a chance that his support—no matter how weak it may be—will be enough to place him first or second, with an opportunity to run in the general sweepstakes. . . .

The runner-up in the first primary often wins the nomination in the second primary, a fact often advanced to support the contention that the popular will would be defeated by awarding nomination to the winner of a plurality in a single primary. The chances are, however, that the result would be the same over the long pull. In the absence of a second primary, the forces that unite behind a single man for that race would join in the first or only primary and produce the same results." *Southern Politics in State and Nation* (1950), pp. 419–422.

names of his opponents. The record in the six cities is indicated in table 14.

The data bear out the claim, but the impact of local conditions is suggested by the differing records of the six cities. When taken as a group, 71 per cent of the incumbents contesting for reëlection were successful. Although the difference of level renders comparison difficult, in 1954, for example, 42 (91 per cent) of the 46 assemblymen who faced opposition in the November election were successful. In 1958, 50 out of 55 assembly incumbents facing November opposition (again 91 per cent), regained office. In neither election was an incumbent assemblyman defeated in the preceding primary. Harris notes that from 1940 through 1950, of the incumbents seeking reëlection, 86 per cent of the congressmen, 95 per cent of the state senators, and 93 per cent of the assemblymen were successful.[10] Incumbents at the municipal level, it would appear, fare somewhat worse in contests for reëlection than their counterparts in the legislature and Congress.

Appointment to Local Office.—More persons originally come to elective local office by appointment to fill a vacancy than is true of state or national offices, where, in California, only United States Senators may be appointed to fill vacancies. In the six cities, the record was as shown in table 15.

TABLE 15

OFFICIALS HOLDING ELECTIVE OFFICE WHO WERE ORIGINALLY
APPOINTED, 1947-1955

City	Holding office		
	Number originally appointed	Total number	Per cent appointees
Chico	0	11	0
Fresno	8	11	73
Pomona	0	11	0
Maywood	2	12	17
San Leandro	4	14	29
Berkeley	6	17	35
TOTAL	20	76	26

The variety of conditions existing in the six cities is indicated by these figures. Taken as a whole, 26 per cent of the mayors and

---

[10] Harris, *California Politics* (1955), p. 41.

councilmen in office in the six cities had originally been appointees. Such vacancies and subsequent council appointments are generally the result of resignations, deaths, and other natural causes. In the past in Berkeley, however, this power of appointment to vacancies had been used as a stratagem of the dominant political group in the community in the retention of power. An incumbent who decided not to seek reëlection would resign a few months before his term expired; the remaining council members then appointed a successor who appeared on the next ballot with the designation "incumbent," providing him an advantage not otherwise possible. The height of this practice was reached in 1940 when the nine-man council included only three persons who had originally been elected to office.

Length of Tenure in Council Office.—This factor in the local election process is, of course, related to incumbency. The record in the six cities is shown in table 16.

TABLE 16

AVERAGE LENGTH OF SERVICE
OF CITY COUNCILMEN, 1947-1955

City	Years
Chico	5.8
Fresno	7.5
Pomona	5.5
Maywood	6.2
San Leandro	6.4
Berkeley	9.6

NOTE: Incumbents in 1955 were credited with the full length of their unexpired term. In Maywood the average would have been 4.7 years, excluding one incumbent with twenty years of service; in Fresno, the average would have been 5.8 years, excluding one councilman with twenty-nine years of service.

A slightly different pattern prevailed for the mayors in the three cities where that office is filled by a separate election. Between 1932 and 1955, the average tenure of mayors was 3.7 years in Pomona, 5.4 years in Berkeley, and 6.0 years in Fresno. In Pomona, the fact that the mayor has only a two-year term whereas the councilmen have four-year terms is an important reason for the relative frequency of turnover. In Fresno, the tenure appears about the same for both offices, while in Berkeley the average term for council personnel is high because of the inclusion in the data of three persons whose service averaged more than twenty years. Excepting these three, the average councilman's term in Berkeley was only 6.5 years.

RECAPITULATION

City election systems are not uniform in California. In some cities each council seat is separately contested. In others, each candidate runs against the entire field, and the two, three, or four highest in the balloting assume office. In some cities mayors are elected separately, in others the mayor's office is filled by the council from among its own membership. Only one election is provided in most cities, but in a few charter communities, runoff contests are required if candidates fail to obtain a majority in the primary election.

There are relatively few examples of uncontested races; there are many examples of close contests and others in which none of the winning candidates are hard pressed. Municipal elections appear to be as competitive, if not more so, as state legislative elections in California.

Of particular importance is the evidence that many candidates are elected by only a plurality; and that in the one city which required runoff contests, the primary leader failed to win the final election in almost one-third of the cases. Given the low turnout in municipal races, the plurality system makes possible the election of candidates with a very small vote, a factor which may seriously affect the representative character of the local council.

As in any system of elections, incumbents in city office have an advantage in a contest for reëlection. On the whole, however, incumbents can probably be defeated somewhat more easily at the local level than at the state and national levels. Local and state races are, of course, hardly comparable. For example, the fact that so many state or U.S. legislative districts have been gerrymandered or are naturally "safe" for one party or the other leads to long tenure if the incumbent and party leadership are so inclined.

Because of the part-time nature of most local offices, vacancies occur frequently; many local officials have originally come to office by appointment rather than election. In California, at least, this is not possible for state legislative offices, and this feature constitutes a marked difference between the two levels. Related to the frequency of vacancies, perhaps, is the pattern of length of service revealed in the six cities. In recent years, council personnel served an average of about six years or one and one-half terms.

6

Groups, Leaders, and Influence

IN ADDITION TO THE STUDY OF FORMALLY DESIGNATED leadership in a society, political science traditionally has examined the organizations and groups active in the political process. The literature frequently discusses pressure groups, lobbies, unofficial decision makers, and the like to describe the role of a large number of organized groups participating in the many activities of the political life of the community, state, or nation.

Formal and continuing organized activity is often absent in California city-election politics. Of the 192 cities replying to the questionnaire, only 25 per cent answered "yes" to the question of whether there were organized groups regularly engaging in the local election process. In almost half of the cities (49 per cent), neither organized nor even informal group activity was reported; most of these cities had a population of less than 25,000. In the six cities, only the Fresno labor unions could be said to meet the description of an identifiable group, publicly and continuously engaged in local election politics.

Despite this lack of formal structure, various community groups are engaged in political activities. These were made the subject of study in both the six-cities and the state-wide survey.

RECRUITMENT OF CANDIDATES AND ORGANIZATION OF THE CAMPAIGN

The lack of formal political structure is best illustrated by the re- cruitment of candidates for city office. In Chico, for example, most recruiting was done by the incumbent councilmen themselves. More than any other group in the community, they had assumed the burden of identifying potential councilmen, not, of course, to compete with themselves but to fill vacancies when they occurred. Selection to the council was often preceded by appointment to an advisory board. Incumbents did not make the search without discussing the qualifications of various potential candidates with friends whose judgment they valued, but there was no group with whom decisions were checked.[1] This pattern had become so well accepted in Chico that it appeared to be a novelty to the community when another avenue of recruitment was successfully used. This method resulted in the election of a woman to the council, the first in more than thirty years. Although she may probably be said to have recruited herself, the encouragement of local women's groups and of her political-party associates was significant in her decision to run.

In larger Fresno, the pattern was similar but with important variations. Here, *individual* members of the commission rather than the body as a whole had undertaken to recruit candidates congenial to their personal views. This had occasionally led to an

---

[1] The questionnaire also provided information on this subject. To the query, "Do incumbents generally play an important role in recruiting new candidates for council office?" 60 per cent of the 192 cities replied yes. Only one of the seven cities of 100,000 population and over so replied, but the remaining positive answers were fairly evenly distributed regardless of the size of the city.

advisory-board appointment before standing for council office, in which event, of course, the entire commission had assumed a voice in the decision. More important had been the urging of personal friends, together with the desire of the candidate to stand for office. In Fresno, the labor unions will probably attempt to see to it that there is always at least one union man on the commission. As in Chico, women's groups, in this instance the American Association of University Women, were responsible for the recruitment of a candidate of their own sex.

Pomona showed a different pattern. There, an informal group of influential business and professional leaders of the community had assumed the responsibility for seeing to it that every two years a "suitable" candidate for mayor (suitable to the downtown group) was recruited and supported. The existence of a perennial mayorality candidate who was anathema to the group was suggested as one reason for this activity. Significantly, however, this interest had rarely carried over to the recruitment of councilmen, which was, as elsewhere, largely the result of personal motivations and the informal encouragement of friends and neighbors. Here, the recent role of one improvement association in recruiting and backing a local candidate was noteworthy, a factor related to the system of district representation in Pomona. The association is not likely to be active except when their representative is up for reëlection.

The influence of the business community (broadly defined, the "economic leaders" of the city) in recruitment was not confined to Pomona. In Berkeley, this group played the dominant role in local politics and was primarily responsible for recruiting a successful mayorality candidate in recent elections. Their influence was frequently exercised through members already on the council with whom they were associated or were congenial. This was often accomplished by the appointment of prospective candidates to council vacancies or to advisory board memberships. At one time, the group sponsored its favored candidates under the label of the Berkeley Council-Manager League; but the name fell into disrepute in 1947 and was not used again.

Other successful candidates in Berkeley were "self-recruited," at times aided by the encouragement of personal friends. One Berkeley woman had been the candidate of organized women's clubs. Of the six cities, only Berkeley had an organization estab-

lished solely to participate in local politics, the Berkeley Municipal League. Formed in 1947 in opposition to the "downtown
slate," the group lost staying power and quickly disappeared.
Berkeley was the only city, too, in which a national political party
organization, the Democrats, appeared as an active force in the
recruitment and support of candidates, and their role was clearly
increasing.

In a manner similar to the "downtown group" active in Berkeley
and Pomona, the "old guard" of business, professional, and land-
owning leaders in San Leandro had constituted an informal and
continuing group for recruiting and supporting candidates over
the years. But the changing political character of rapidly expanding San Leandro had so altered the role of this group that its
future direction and activity were uncertain. With the implementation of a district system of representation, local improvement
associations appeared to have an ever-increasing place in the recruitment and support of candidates. The activity of incumbents
in the recruitment process, necessitated by a series of council
vacancies, was also important.

In tiny Maywood, it would have been surprising to find any
evidence of political structure. Politics during the past decade
had centered on a single dominant personality who had recruited candidates or by his actions caused opposing candidates
to enter the field. His defeat in the late 1950's suggested, however, that new forces were entering the picture.

Problems of Recruitment.—Although no question in the written
canvass of cities related specifically to recruitment, no other subject elicited more reaction from the respondents in their written
comments. Almost all stressed the difficulty of attracting able men
to stand for public office.

Factors cited as producing the difficulty included the public
and newspaper abuse which local officials had to undergo, the
fear stands on public issues would damage the incumbent's business, and the loss of time with inadequate or no remuneration.
Typical of the comments was this one from a city of 25,000:

> It is very difficult to get a good businessman to run for city
> office. The press constantly criticizes every action of the
> council and in so doing certainly does not stimulate any
> interest in city government. Most people simply will not

take the beating created by such a situation and as there is no compensation for the hours and hours of work there naturally is no attraction.

From another city came this observation:

Public apathy is the main problem. Councilmen run as a civic duty and usually suffer to some extent financially, and so generally (in a small city) are not too aggressive, and do not pretend to assume political leadership.

This example was cited by another:

A group of businessmen called upon six qualified people to become candidates for mayor; all refused.

In the absence of a formal mechanism, this method of recruiting was described by this respondent from a city of 10,000:

A few people get together around a table in a restaurant drinking coffee and decide they are going to run someone and that's the way it goes, good, bad, or indifferent makes no difference, never taking into consideration his background, training, or education. As a result we get men who talk in nickels and dimes, when we need men who understand terms of $1,000 and up.

Another stated:

There have been few, if any, issues in the city elections over the past several years. There have been no groups advocating a particular slate of candidates for office. In fact it has been difficult to induce good men to run for offices. Usually the present city council or members of the Chamber of Commerce will pick an outstanding man and ask him to run. He has never failed to be elected.

The need for a more formal method of recruiting and supporting candidates was expressed by this respondent from a community of 40,000:

The principal problem here is that there is little or no deliberate effort to select and enlist a field of top quality candidates for Council positions. That is no reflection on either those who run or those who are elected—but these are generally rounded up and "pressured" at the last minute to become candidates, when many times a more deliberate selection of candidates would produce people who are better acquainted with the community and more able to give the time and attention required. At other times when some care is taken to select candidates, they are not given the amount of support necessary to assure their election. I have always thought that a continuing group of citizens concerned only with the best interests of the community should concern themselves with the recruitment and support of candidates at each city election. Otherwise, many times the positions are filled by default rather than deliberate judgment.

Several cities reported the existence of such a continuing and interested group, generally informal, in these statements:

[A city of 100,000]: A small but strong group of most representative citizens urge capable and competent people to run, circulate their petitions, make all the speeches and completely finance the campaign. I have never known any member of the group to reflect a selfish interest either before, during or after the campaign. It is a most unique format, and the group's candidates have been successful for 25 years.

[A city of 30,000]: For the past twelve years or so councilmanic elections have been dominated by a loosely organized group that started out with the name_____. For a year or two this organization held meetings and elected officers. Since that time, the group gets together two or three months before election and either endorses candidates already in the field or tries to induce persons they favor to run for office. The group raises funds to support candidates of their choice but discourages, in fact will not accept, large contributions from any source. The usual contribution is $25. Both Democrats and Republicans belong to this organization and, to the best of my knowledge, party affiliation has never been a factor in city elections. As far as I can recollect, this organization has not backed a loser since its inception. Their support may not always be necessary to be elected but their opposition is certainly to be reckoned with. Membership changes according to the man and issues involved. There are no officers at present and no dues. Opposition to this group has, in recent years, come largely from retired people and from what might be termed the "anti" group.

[A city of 25,000]: Men are encouraged to run for City Council at the insistence of an informal group of representative businessmen from industry and commerce. Generally about 15 or 20 men attend these meetings. They decide who to ask to run and the individual selected is generally a successful businessman. He is approached on the basis that the time has arrived for him to pay his debt to "God and Country." This appears to be the only way that you can interest men of ability to seek office. The campaign money is raised by one of the committee who pays all bills and does not disclose to anyone, particularly the candidates, the source of his funds. It would be much more satisfactory if men of ability would seek to serve their community on their own initiative. Each man then could be an individual candidate and not a part of a slate. . . . One drawback to the non-paid feature of council office is that it may stop the low salaried worker from running for a Council seat. He could not afford it because each Councilman spends about 4 hours a week, not counting luncheons, etc. at the City Hall during working hours.

All councilmen in office in these three cities with formalized recruiting mechanisms were registered Republicans. The two larger cities are themselves strongly Republican, while the third is evenly split between the two parties. It may be possible that: (1) Such formalized recruiting activity, which relies heavily on the support of business groups, may take place more often in communities with strong Republican majorities; (2) the recruiting activities of groups, which are Republican because of their business membership, focus on persons from similar walks of life who are, incidentally, Republicans.

RELATIVE IMPORTANCE OF COMMUNITY GROUPS

A key question asked of city respondents in the state-wide questionnaire was designed to discover which groups in the community were considered important in local politics: "If someone wished to run for election to your city council, the support (public or behind the scenes) of which of the following persons or groups would be most helpful to his success? Please indicate first, second, third, etc. in importance." Then followed a list of twenty-three groups, such as realtors, women's organizations, and the local newspaper, space to insert the requested number and a line marked "Other" where groups not listed might be inserted. The frequency with which these groups were cited is indicated in the following table. Although the answers to such a question are inherently subjective, they constitute an informed review of the general picture in the state.

Two groups head the state-wide list: the local newspaper and merchants. They were listed in 67 per cent and 62 per cent of all the cities; when listed, their support was regarded favorably as indicated by the relatively high percentage of first choice and first to third choice "votes." Service clubs and women's organizations were listed as helpful in more than half of the 192 cities respond-

TABLE 17

RATING OF IMPORTANCE OF LOCAL GROUPS IN CITY COUNCIL RACES

	Per cent of 192 cities		
Group	Some importance	1st to 3d in importance	1st in importance
Local newspaper	67	51	23
Merchants	62	48	24
Service clubs	58	35	11
Women's organizations	55	29	6
Veterans' groups	40	10	3
Lay church groups	36	14	6
Improvement associations	33	19	8
City employees	24	9	3
Labor unions	22	6	3
Ministers	21	5	1
Teachers	21	6	0.5
Realtors	19	8	0.5
Masonic Lodge	18	6	0.5
Other lodges	15	4	0.5
Bankers	14	5	2
Attorneys	12	4	0.5
Political party organizations	10	3	2
Contractors	9	3	0.5
Manufacturers	8	4	0.5
Doctors and dentists	5	0.5	0
Liquor dealers, bartenders	3	2	0
Public utilities	2	0.5	0

NOTE: No limit was placed on the number of groups a respondent could check; but not more than ten were included in the tabulations. The columns are not mutually exclusive. A group listed first in importance, for example, is counted in all three columns.

ing and as first to third in importance in approximately one-third of the cities. A third cluster of groups listed as helpful in at least one-third of the cities included veterans groups, lay church groups, and improvement associations. However, the frequency with which these were cited as first or first to third in importance was far less than the four previously mentioned groups. In 58 per cent of the cities where improvement associations were mentioned, however, they tended to be rated first to third in importance, a much higher ratio than that of other than the top four groups.

Mentioned far less frequently, particularly in the first or first to third choice categories, fall the remaining groups. The table records the frequency with which a group was mentioned in all cities, not the group's importance in a particular city. Although contractors, for example, are listed last among the groups mentioned as "first in importance," they were listed as a dominant group in one city.

It is not surprising, of course, to find that groups are listed in different orders of frequency depending on the size of the city.[2] For example, only six groups are listed as helpful in 20 per cent or more of the cities with a population of less than 5,000, as compared to at least eleven groups in the larger cities. In table 18, the information described above is treated separately for each class of cities, grouped according to population.

The Local Press.—The local newspaper was considered helpful in 67 per cent of cities of all sizes, being mentioned in from 58 per cent to 88 per cent of the cities in the various population classes in addition to the two cities of more than 250,000. The paper tended to be rated more often and valued more highly in cities of more than 25,000, as suggested by the figures in table 19.[3]

---

[2] Several respondents, particularly from small cities, stated that this part of the questionnaire (in some cases the entire questionnaire) had little application to their community. Typical of the remarks made was this one: "In a city this size [population 2,350], we do not have any party or group participation to any great extent. Most candidates run as individuals who very rarely have any support except what few friends they have to work for them." From a larger city (35,000) came a similar comment: "In my experience it has been individuals who have concerned themselves with local elections rather than any of the particular groups which you mention. Their efforts also have been variable rather than confined to any particular issue."

[3] The questionnaire failed to discriminate between cities which did not have a local newspaper and those which did have but in which the paper was rated of no importance. A question aimed only at those cities which actually had a local paper would have been of more value, although difficulties of isolating this factor in metropolitan communities would clearly exist.

TABLE 18

Local Groups Considered Important in Winning a City Council Race in Cities of Varying Sizes
(In Per cent of Cities)

Local group	0-4,999 (53 cities) Some importance	0-4,999 1st to 3d in importance	5,000-9,999 (37 cities) Some importance	5,000-9,999 1st to 3d in importance	10,000-24,999 (57 cities) Some importance	10,000-24,999 1st to 3d in importance	25,000-49,999 (25 cities) Some importance	25,000-49,999 1st to 3d in importance	50,000-99,999 (13 cities) Some importance	50,000-99,999 1st to 3d in importance	100,000-249,999 (5 cities) Some importance	100,000-249,999 1st to 3d in importance	250,000-499,999 (one city) Some importance	250,000-499,999 1st to 3d in importance	500,000 and more (one city) Some importance	500,000 and more 1st to 3d in importance
Newspapers	58	40	68	46	63	49	88	76	77	69	60	40	100	100	100	100
Merchants clubs	66	58	70	65	58	42	60	24	46	31	40	40	100	0	100	100
Service clubs	58	43	73	54	56	25	56	24	46	31	20	0	0	0	0	0
Women's organizations	49	28	49	14	56	32	68	52	62	31	40	20	100	0	100	0
Veterans	42	13	38	8	32	7	56	16	46	7	40	0	0	0	100	0
Lay church groups	42	28	46	16	25	0	32	8	38	23	40	20	100	0	0	0
Improvement associations	15	8	22	5	40	28	60	44	38	23	40	20	100	0	100	0
City employees	17	6	22	11	19	9	52	16	31	8	40	0	0	0	0	0
Labor unions	9	4	19	3	25	7	28	4	54	23	20	0	100	0	100	0
Ministers	9	8	27	5	23	2	32	4	23	8	20	0	0	0	0	0
Teachers	13	4	24	5	19	4	36	16	31	15	0	0	0	0	0	0
Realtors	0	0	40	8	0	0	36	8	38	12	20	20	0	0	100	0
Masonic lodge	13	4	22	8	23	11	16	0	0	0	20	0	100	0	0	0
Other lodges	11	0	0	0	24	0	0	0	0	0	0	0	0	0	0	0
Bankers	9	0	19	0	0	0	16	0	0	0	20	0	0	0	100	0
Attorneys	0	0	0	0	21	0	0	0	0	0	0	0	0	0	0	0
Political party	0	0	0	0	0	0	28	0	0	0	0	0	0	0	100	0
Manufacturers	9	0	0	0	0	0	0	0	23	0	20	0	0	0	100	0

Respondents were also questioned on the role of the local press in the city campaigns: "Does the local press support or endorse candidates for city office?" In 76 (40 per cent) of the 192 cities it was indicated that such activity took place in "every election" or in "many elections," while in another 25 per cent activity in "few

TABLE 19

IMPORTANCE OF NEWSPAPERS IN CITY COUNCIL RACES

		Per cent of cities	
Size of city	Total number of cities	Some importance	1st to 3d in importance
Less than 25,000	147	63	45
25,000 and more	45	82	71
TOTAL	192	67	51

elections" was reported. The larger the city, the more likely was an affirmative answer. For example, the "every" or "many" reply was reported in 32 per cent of the cities of less than 25,000, contrasted with 64 per cent of the cities of more than 25,000. (As noted, this may simply have been the result of the absence of any local paper in many small cities.) The record of the press in supporting successful candidates was impressive. Of the 124 cities in which local press support or endorsements were given at all, in 89 (72 per cent) the candidates supported by the paper reportedly "always won" or "won many times" and in another 25 per cent supported candidates "occasionally won." This successful press record, either in pushing candidates to victory or in supporting candidates who would have won anyway, was indicated regardless of the size of the city, but particularly in larger cities. In 70 per cent of the cities with a population of less than 50,000 in which the press was reported active, and in 95 per cent of the cities of more than 50,000, candidates supported by the paper reportedly won "many times" or "always."

In the six cities separately investigated, the activity of the local press varied considerably. Only in San Leandro and Fresno were the daily papers actively and editorially engaged in local politics. In these two cities, too, the impact of growth had created thousands of readers who found information and guidance in the paper to offset their newness to the community. In Chico and Pomona, the two papers played a much less positive role, particularly with reference to local elections. In Berkeley, the newspaper, perhaps hampered by its metropolitan competition, appeared to have abdicated its potential role for community leadership. Presumably, however, its endorsements for council office were important to those elements of the community that constituted its main body of readers. In retrospect, the existence in San Leandro and Fresno of an energetic and independent press appeared to do much to set the tone and pace of local politics—a tone and pace, it may be added, that seemed desirable.[4]

Merchants Groups.—Only slightly less important in terms of frequency mentioned was the merchants' group, listed as helpful in at least 40 per cent of the cities in each population class, the range varying from 40 to 70 per cent in addition to the two cities of more than 250,000. Unlike the local newspaper, however, the merchants tended to be mentioned as helpful and important more frequently in cities of less than 25,000, as suggested by the figures in table 20:

TABLE 20

IMPORTANCE OF MERCHANTS IN CITY COUNCIL RACES

| | | Per cent of cities | |
Size of city	Total number of cities	Some importance	1st to 3d in importance
Less than 10,000	90	68	61
10,000-25,000	57	58	42
25,000 and more	45	56	29
TOTAL	192	62	51

[4] It has been suggested that the local newspaper plays a larger role under a nonpartisan system of elections. Referring to both the state and local scene in California, one text states: "Denied the emblem of party, both through the adoption of nonpartisanship for all local, school, and judicial offices, and through the deceptive practice of cross-filing, the voter has been forced to grope through the excessively long ballot without proper aid. The average man is confronted with a task that staggers the most alert citizen, and must pick up his civic data in a haphazard way. The newspapers thereby secure a great boost in political influence, and so do those who can hire the principal media for disseminating information." Crouch *et al., State and Local Government in California* (1952), p. 43.

While this generalization may be true, the role of the press in a community cannot be so readily assessed. The size and growth of the community and the character of the paper come readily to mind as factors to be considered.

Almost as large a proportion of cities in each size classification listed merchants as of some importance, but there is a sharp decline in the number of cities that regarded the support of this group as especially important. As can be seen, merchants were listed and considered important most frequently in the small cities of the state.[5]

In the six cities, several reasons were advanced to explain the dominant role of business in recruiting activities. First, local government has an important effect on the welfare of the business community. Taxes, zoning, traffic control, and parking can often mean the difference between profit and loss to merchants, realtors, and related banking and legal interests. Hence, the business community seeks influence over the city council in a more consistent fashion than other community groups. Secondly, the commercial interests possess important sources of communication, internal and external. The service clubs, the chamber of commerce, and other business-related organizations provide frequent and important points of contact at which opinions and attitudes on local politics and candidates are a normal topic of conversation. At the same time, many of this group are also in positions where their opinions are solicited by others outside the immediate interest group. The net effect of this communications system is to provide the business community with "natural" advantages in the political process not possessed by other groups.[6] Thirdly, it was

---

[5] Typical of several comments concerning the role of the business community in local politics was this one from a respondent in a small town (population 6,000): "In a small town, your councilmen generally come from one source, the business community. Either the officials are active at present in business or else they are retired businessmen. Party politics have no importance though it is more likely the councilman will be a Republican because most businessmen seem to be Republicans. Two of the councilmen now are Democrats, although I doubt that many people know it. Your councilmen just aren't active in partisan politics. During a campaign, the candidates get support on a personal basis (i.e., fellow church members, Rotarians, Elks, etc.). With a registered vote of 2,600 and typically a 60 per cent turnout, it doesn't take too much to know a majority of the voters who actually cast ballots. At least on a small town basis, this system works well. I am sure, though, when the town grows, there will be changes—not to party politics, but to a point where the 'old-timers' will be joined by some 'newcomers' from the non-business community in conducting the town's affairs."

[6] A good description of this "natural" communications system is suggested by Berelson in discussing Elmira: "An important circumstance making for greater political harmony within the business group is simply their greater rate of political activity within the community. They belong to more organizations than the labor group, they talk politics more, and they are looked to more for political advice. They not only reassure themselves through such activities; they also set a political 'tone' for the entire community. And they were in positions to

suggested, in communities where campaigns are costly, the business community commands financial resources far superior to most. Lastly, only well-to-do business and professional men, or those in occupations in which public service is good advertising (e.g., insurance), or retired persons can afford to stand for and serve their city in elected office.

Service Clubs.—Service clubs also are more important in the

TABLE 21

IMPORTANCE OF SERVICE CLUBS IN CITY COUNCIL RACES

| | | Per cent of cities | |
| | Total number | Some | 1st to 3d in |
Size of city	of cities	importance	importance
Less than 5,000	53	58	43
5,000-10,000	37	73	54
10,000-25,000	57	56	25
25,000-50,000	25	56	24
50,000 and more	20	35	20
TOTAL	192	58	35

do so; about 80 per cent of the occupational elite of the community were Republicans and about 75 per cent of the officers of clubs and organizations." Berelson *et al.*, *Voting* (1954), p. 57.

In a much broader context, Lipset explains the consistent voting of the "higher economic classes" in terms of "the higher degree of organization and the greater facilities for communication possessed by the upper classes." Lipset *et al.*, "The Psychology of Voting: An Analysis of Political Behavior," *in* Lindzey, ed., *Handbook of Social Psychology* (1954), II, 1141.

Ramsey discusses the role of the business leadership in Detroit, which also employs a nonpartisan ballot for city office, in these terms: "The interlocking nature of the civic associations, the excellence of their leadership, and the fact that they refrained from the appearance of attempting to dictate or of self-interest combined to make them the most effective pressure group in the city . . . their breadth and diversity gave them a vitality ordinarily lacking in such organizations." These civic associations "were basically committed to Republican policies and were under the control of men who were in some cases openly active in Republican circles." Ramsey, "Some Aspects of Nonpartisan Government in Detroit, 1918-1940" (1944), pp. 292, 163. See also p. 100.

However, a recent study of an English town of 20,000 reports that "none of the three business groups in Glossop plays a very active role in the public life of the town. They are largely immersed in their own internal affairs and social activities, and when they engage in political or industrial controversies or negotiations their dealings are more likely to be with bodies outside the town than with those within it. . . . This reflects the increasing importance of functional organization in British society, and the accompanying decline in the importance of the local community as a focus of decision-making activities." Birch, *Small-Town Politics: A Study of Political Life in Glossop* (1959), p. 167.

very small cities of the state, particularly in those with a population of from 5,000 to 10,000.

Among the six cities, too, service-club membership was found to be politically more important in the smaller communities.[7]

Cities in the 10,000–25,000 group mentioned the service clubs and merchants as of some importance almost the same number of times, 58 per cent for the merchants and 56 per cent for the service clubs. But merchants were rated first to third in importance in 42 per cent of the cities of this size, service clubs in only 25 per cent. This difference is less pronounced in the cities of less than 10,000. In both groups of cities, however, the frequency with which service clubs were mentioned fell below that of the merchants, who comprise a good share of the membership. However, not all towns necessarily have active service clubs, and the lack of response to this item may indicate not the weakness of the clubs in the city but simply their absence. Also, many clubs traditionally do not participate in local politics, not even informally.

Women's Organizations.—Women's organizations were indicated as important in cities of all sizes, most frequently, 68 per cent, in communities of 25,000 to 100,000, where only the local paper was cited more often. In no population group were the ladies' groups mentioned by less than 40 per cent of the cities.

Despite this widespread indication of importance, in only four instances were women's organizations noted as formally or informally active in the recruitment and active support of candidates. In the six cities, the difference is represented by the contrasting situation in Pomona and Fresno. In the latter city, motivated by the issue of women's representation, the American Association of University Women actively recruited and was primarily responsible for the election of Fresno's first woman commissioner. To a lesser degree, similar experiences were reported in Berkeley and

---

[7] Hollingshead cites an instance of service-club dominance in his account of life in a town of 6,200: "Responsibility for the operation of the Elmtown school system rests in the hands of a seven-man Board of Education. . . . Theoretically, any adult citizen in the district may be a candidate for the school board, and if he receives enough votes, elected. In practice, the members of the Board of Education come mainly from the two upper classes and have to qualify under informal ground rules. Even to be considered for the Board a person has to be male, Protestant, Republican, a property owner, preferably a Rotarian, or at least approved by the Rotarians. (Rotarians are proud of the way they have controlled the selection of the Board for more than twenty-five years.)" Hollingshead, *Elmtown's Youth* (1949), p. 123.

Chico. In Pomona, on the other hand, the politically active women's organizations served as the machinery to implement the almost always male choices of the downtown business community. The evidence would suggest that, in the infrequent instances when the ladies wish to, they can generally elect one of their own. In any election, their support is important.

Veterans.—Veterans' organizations were cited as helpful in 40 per cent of the total number of cities, but were considered of first to third importance in only 10 per cent of the cities. There appeared to be no meaningful relationship between size of the city and the frequency with which veterans were listed. In the six cities, also, veterans appeared to be a secondary group in importance, rarely recruiting or campaigning for a candidate in their own right but being frequently cited as of value in the informal word-of-mouth campaigning characteristic of local politics.

Lay Church Groups.—Lay church groups were mentioned and cited as important most frequently in cities of less than 10,000, as shown in table 22.

TABLE 22

IMPORTANCE OF LAY CHURCH GROUPS IN CITY COUNCIL RACES

Size of city	Total number of cities	Per cent of cities	
		Some importance	1st to 3d in importance
Less than 10,000	53	43	23
10,000 and more	139	29	6
TOTAL	192	36	14

Only in the "under 10,000" group, also, were lay church groups cited as of first importance among the community groups, eleven (12 per cent) of the cities of this size so listing them.

The record of the six cities indicated a far more pervading influence for religious organizations. In Fresno, the vice question had brought the churches and their ministers openly into the political process. In Pomona, the religious origins and traditions of the city and the continued activity of the churches had made them the center of much of the social life of a segment of the community, and the informal political activity resulting from these associations was important. (The continued existence of the wet-dry issue in Pomona was important in this regard.) A similar situation applied in Chico, while in Maywood, the dominance of the Mormon community had been a factor of unique political importance. There, the town's leading politician, a Mormon, had used his church affiliation and church-related groups to significant advantage.

Improvement Associations.—Improvement associations were also cited in a widely varying frequency depending on the size of city. Mentioned as helpful by one-third of all the cities, their listing in the various classifications varied from 15 to 60 per cent, in addition to the two cities above 250,000. In almost 60 per cent of the cases where improvement associations were listed, they were cited as first to third in importance. They were mentioned most frequently in cities of the 25,000–50,000 classification and as first in importance in 24 per cent of these cities.

TABLE 23

IMPORTANCE OF IMPROVEMENT ASSOCIATIONS IN CITY COUNCIL RACES

		Per cent of cities	
Size of city	Total number of cities	Some importance	1st to 3d in importance
Less than 25,000	147	26	15
25,000–50,000	25	60	44
50,000 and more	20	45	20
TOTAL	192	33	19

Similar findings resulted from the six cities study. Only in Pomona and San Leandro had the local neighborhood groups taken an active part in local election politics, but their influence had been great. In San Leandro, particularly, overnight development of agricultural land into large subdivisions, each with a self-consciousness and identity, had thrust the improvement associations into a special place of prominence in the local political scene. In fact, a good share of community politics was destined, at least in the immediate future, to revolve around the internal politics of the several associations and their relationships with each other.

Other Groups.—Other than the above seven groups, no group was listed as helpful in the state-wide survey by more than one-quarter of the 192 participating cities or as first to third in importance in more than 10 per cent. Although the number of cities at times becomes too small to permit meaningful analysis, the following observations may be made. (Note, again, that nonmentioning of a group in many cities does not indicate its lack of importance in a particular city.)

City employees, listed in 24 per cent of all the cities, were reported as helpful in 19 per cent of cities under 25,000, and 42 per cent of cities over that figure. The group only infrequently was rated as first to third in importance.[8]

Labor unions were mentioned as helpful in only 9 per cent of the cities under 5,000, 24 per cent of the cities from 5,000 to 50,000, and in 50 per cent of the cities over 50,000, including the two cities of more than 250,000. In 28 cities, 16 per cent of those under 100,000, respondents stated that public support of labor *hurt* a candidate's chances. It is obvious that this impression is even more speculative than one indicating whether a group's support would prove helpful; whether an accurate appraisal or not, the reported expressions of opinion are revealing.

In Berkeley a union official sat on the city council, but only in Fresno of the six cities was organized labor important in the local political scene. There, commencing in 1947, unions had successfully recruited and elected a commission candidate to what is now often referred to as the "labor seat."

Ministers (listed in 21 per cent of the cities) were cited more frequently in the smaller communities and by only one city over 100,000. Table 24 compares the frequency with which ministers were listed to that of the lay church groups.

The social role of small-town churches may explain the differ-

---

[8] In at least one large California community, the participation of municipal employees in the political life of the city is considered of importance and concern to local leaders, as indicated by this statement of a respondent: "The important thing to me is that the firemen and policemen and the various public works employees who are organized under AFL can make financial contributions by their dues to the candidacy of a councilman, can publicly indicate their preference for council candidates and through asking people to support labor's candidates exert their influence on election of officials who set their rates of pay and working conditions. This, to me, is basically and tragically wrong. . . . As in most California cities today, our worst 'pressure groups' are city employees."

ence between the frequency of lay church and ministerial activity in the smaller cities, particularly those under 5,000.[9]

TABLE 24

COMPARISON OF IMPORTANCE OF LAY CHURCH GROUPS AND MINISTERS

Size of city	Total number of cities	Per cent of cities	
		Lay church group	Ministers
Less than 5,000	53	42	9
5,000-10,000	37	46	27
10,000 and more	102	29	25
TOTAL	192	36	21

NOTE: Comparison based on cities listing group as "of some importance."

Teachers were listed as helpful in 13 per cent of the cities under 5,000, in 25 per cent of the cities between 5,000 and 100,000, and in none of the seven cities with a population of 100,000 or more.

Realtors, listed as helpful in 19 per cent of all cities, were mentioned in only 6 per cent of the cities under 5,000, in 25 per cent of the cities from 5,000 to 100,000, and in two (29 per cent) of the seven cities over 100,000. The frequency with which the *Masonic Lodge* was cited, on the other hand, was consistently distributed regardless of size, 18 per cent of the cities under 100,-000 listing its support as helpful in addition to one city over 100,000. No other group included in the questionnaire was cited by more than 15 per cent of the cities.[10]

---

[9] Respondents in five cities of the state reported that the public support of ministers as a group had proved damaging in recent years. Typical was this comment from a small rural community: "The local ministerial association, I should say a portion of that association, tried to run a group of candidates via a write-in campaign some four years ago. They were defeated more by their own tactics than any other reason."

[10] Other groups than those described above are important in particular cities. One of the most unique was described by a respondent from a small town: "It's almost a fixation here that no one or at least very few can be elected to the city council unless they are members of the volunteer fire department. The fire department has a hard core, closed, loyal membership of 75, which together with an auxiliary of women and cross-memberships in service clubs, veterans' organizations and civic groups gives them a virtual control in city elections. Of the five members of the city council today, all are firemen, three are past chiefs and the mayors of this city have been past chiefs for a generation. City council elections are considered a stepping-stone for alert, active firemen. The fire department usually gathers the more active and aggressive men of the city, through not only a fire fighting, but a social organization; coupled with the members that have gone on the 'honorary list' in past years, the 100-year-old Fire Department has a sizable

Groups Whose Public Support Would Be Damaging—In answer
to the question, "Are there any groups in the above list whose
public support would *hurt* a candidate's chances?" [11] only four
groups were mentioned with any frequency: liquor dealers and
bartenders, listed by 49 per cent of the 192 cities; labor unions,
mentioned above, listed by 15 per cent; political party organizations, listed by 12 per cent and public utilities, listed by 11 per
cent. Table 25 distributes these replies by size of city.

TABLE 25

GROUPS WHOSE PUBLIC SUPPORT WAS CONSIDERED HARMFUL
IN CITY COUNCIL RACES

Size of city	Total number of cities	Per cent of cities listing as harmful:			
		Liquor dealers, bartenders	Union labor	Political party	Public utility
Less than 5,000	53	30	8	6	6
5,000-10,000	37	49	14	16	5
10,000-25,000	57	58	21	7	16
25,000-50,000	25	64	20	16	24
50,000-100,000	13	69	15	23	8
100,000-250,000	5	40	0	40	20
250,000-500,000	1	100	0	100	0
500,000-1,000,000	0	0	0	0	0
1,000,000 and more	1	0	0	0	0
TOTAL	192	49	15	12	11

Local factors and circumstances unquestionably dictated the
listing of one or more of these groups in a community. For example the support of liquor dealers and bartenders is not regarded
as harshly in cities under 5,000 as in the larger communities. In

---

wad of potential votes and a running start on city leadership." No other single
formal group in any of the cities responding appeared to be as active and influential as that described here.

---

[11] The first question, of which this was part *b* contained some ambiguity, which,
however, does not appear to have been troublesome. Question 1*a* called for an
indication of groups whose "public or behind-the-scenes" support would be
helpful to a candidate; question 1*b* asked for an indication of groups whose
"public support" would be harmful. There could well be groups whose "behind-
the-scenes" support would be helpful, but whose "public" support would be
damaging. The format of the questionnaire probably discouraged clarification of
this point, and no attempt was made in the coding to describe this possibility in
the very few cases where it appeared to occur.

a very small town, knowing the proprietor and his reputation are perhaps more important than his occupation.

ORGANIZED GROUP ACTIVITY IN LOCAL ELECTIONS

The first questions in the state-wide survey attempted to determine the groups in the community whose support was considered to be helpful (or damaging) to a candidate in a local campaign. The second group of questions solicited opinions on the extent of organized activity in the local election process: "Are there in your city any organized groups, such as a civic league, good government association, or labor union, that regularly put forward or endorse city council candidates, prepare and circulate campaign literature, or engage in similar public political activities?"

Unlike answers to the preceding questions, which required a subjective appraisal, answers to this inquiry were supposedly based on a specific and readily observable factual situation.

As noted above, only 49 (25 per cent) of the 192 cities indicated the existence of organized activity in their community. There was a distinct relationship, as might be expected, between the size of the city and an affirmative reply.[12] (See table 26.)

---

[12] Respondents from council-manager cities more often reported organized activity than did those from mayor-council cities. In the cities of less than 5,000, there were too few council-manager cities, and in cities of more than 25,000, too few mayor-council cities, to make analysis of these groups meaningful. However, in the 5,000-to-25,000 classification, these results were reported:

EXISTENCE OF ORGANIZED POLITICAL ACTIVITY
(By Form of Government and Size of City)

Form of government	5,000-10,000 population			10,000-25,000 population		
	Total number of cities	Cities reporting organized activity		Total number of cities	Cities reporting organized activity	
		Number	Per cent		Number	Per cent
Council-manager	14	4	29	42	12	29
Mayor-council	23	3	13	15	3	20

It may be that activity essential to the adoption of the council-manager plan in the first instance is indicative of continued organized local political activity in the life of the community. There are not sufficient data to do more than suggest this as a subject for further investigation.

low organization

TABLE 26

CITIES INDICATING ORGANIZED ACTIVITY

Size of city	Total number of cities	Per cent
Less than 5,000	53	11
5,000-25,000	94	28
25,000 and more	45	50
TOTAL	192	25

In the 49 cities, 65 different groups were named. Of these:

Sixteen (25 per cent) could be classed as business groups: merchants, business and professional men, chambers of commerce, service clubs. All these groups were reported in cities below 100,000.

Sixteen (25 per cent) were classed as "all elements of the community" or a "cross-section." These groups were found in every size of city except the two over 250,000.

Eleven (17 per cent) were classed as organized labor or labor unions. None of these groups was in a city below 5,000 but they were active in both cities over 250,000. In five of the seven cities over 100,000, no regular organized activity other than that of labor-union groups was reported.

Twenty-two (33 per cent) were classified as miscellaneous. These included property owners' associations, church groups, old timers, active in cities of all sizes below 100,000.

The respondents' answers to the question, "Are the candidates of this group successful?" indicated the pattern in table 27:[13]

---

[13] "Successful" or not, there was not always agreement between two respondents from the same area concerning the manners and morals of groups active in the local political process. One Republican county chairman wrote, "We have an organization that call themselves the Good Government Committee, that are made up of a group that are more or less radicals. They try to get their own candidates into office by confusing the voters, both on city and school elections." However, a city official from the identical community described the scene in these terms: "As a result of squabbles over the council-manager plan, a Good Government Committee was founded which was definitely not based on any party affiliation and they, along with women's clubs sponsored charter amendments to strengthen the system and recruited and elected candidates."

TABLE 27

SUCCESS OF CANDIDATES SUPPORTED BY ORGANIZED GROUP ACTIVITY

Group	Number of cities in which group active	Per cent of cities in which supported candidate was:		
		Frequently successful	Sometimes successful	Total
"Cross-section"	16	69	25	94
Business	16	44	38	82
Miscellaneous	22	41	32	73
Labor union	11	18	64	82

INFORMAL GROUP ACTIVITY IN LOCAL ELECTIONS

A question similar to that on organized activity asked, "Are there in your city any *informal* groups of citizens that *regularly* get to-

TABLE 28

CITIES INDICATING INFORMAL ACTIVITY

Size of city	Total number of cities	Per cent
Less than 5,000	53	21
5,000-50,000	119	42
50,000 and more	20	75
TOTAL	192	40

gether before each city election to recruit candidates, donate money for campaigning, provide personal support, or the like?" [14]

Of the 192 cities, 76 (40 per cent) reported the existence of

---

[14] It was intended that the two questions, one referring to organized groups and the second to informal groups, would be considered as mutually exclusive, that one group would not be—except in rare instances—considered active in both a formal and informal fashion. It is clear, however, that in a few cases this intention was not clear, so that the same group was reported active in both answers. Where this was obvious, the more correct reply was used; where the intent of the respondent could not be clearly ascertained, both answers were recorded, even though only one reply was probably proper.

such informal activity, especially in the larger cities, as indicated in table 28.[15]

In the 76 cities, 95 different groups were named. Of these:

Fifty-eight (61 per cent) could be described as business groups: merchants, bankers, professional men, realtors, and the like. These groups were found in every size of city, but were least reported in the very small cities. In only 9 per cent of the cities under 5,000 was such activity reported, as compared with 38 per cent of the cities above this size, including both cities over 250,000.

Seven (8 per cent) were classed as "general" or "cross-section." These were, with one exception, in the 5,000-25,-000 class.

Five (5 per cent) included farmers. These were reported only in cities from 10,000 to 50,000. (Two of these groups were associated with business groups listed above.)

Five (5 per cent) had union labor membership. These were reported only in cities from 50,000 to 250,000. (One of these groups was associated with business groups listed above.)

Twenty (21 per cent) included miscellaneous elements, not separately tabulated: improvement associations, church groups, veterans, and others. Such groups were reported in cities of all sizes under 100,000. (Four of these were associated with business groups listed above.)

---

[15] As with organized group activity reported above, respondents more often reported informal activity in council-manager cities than in those of the mayor-council type:

EXISTENCE OF INFORMAL POLITICAL ACTIVITY
(By Form of Government and Size of City)

Form of government	5,000-10,000 population			10,000-25,000 population		
	Total number of cities	Cities reporting informal activity		Total number of cities	Cities reporting informal activity	
		Number	Per cent		Number	Per cent
Council-manager	14	7	50	42	21	50
Mayor-council	23	9	39	15	2	13

As conjectured above, if the relationship suggested by the admittedly slim evidence does in fact exist, it may indicate that the forces which are active in a community in the adoption of the manager plan may continue active in later elections.

Removing the impact of the duplications, in 58 (76 per cent) of the 76 cities in which informal activity was reported, business elements of the community wholly or partially comprised the membership of the informal group. Such business activity was likely to be important as evidenced by these responses to the inquiry, "Are the candidates of this group successful?"

TABLE 29

SUCCESS OF CANDIDATES SUPPORTED BY INFORMAL GROUP ACTIVITY

Group	Number of cities in which group active	Per cent of cities in which supported candidate was:		
		Frequently successful	Sometimes successful	Total
Business	58	83	16	99
Farmers	5	80	20	100
"Cross-section"	7	71	29	100
Miscellaneous	20	60	15	75
Labor union	5	0	40	40

Did cities which reported the existence of organized activity also report informal activity? How many cities, on the other hand, reported no activity at all, organized or informal?[16] The pattern in the 192 cities was as follows: 15 per cent reported both types of activity; 49 per cent neither type; 11 per cent only organized activity; 25 per cent only informal activity. The larger the city the more both types of activity were reported; the smaller the city, the greater the chance that neither would be indicated:

---

[16] Several respondents took the opportunity to comment on the status and extent of organized or informal activity in their cities. One noted that in his town the support of organizations was resented by the voters. Several others commented that in a small town voters knew candidates personally, implying that no intervening organized apparatus was necessary. However, a different group stressed the need for organized activity in recruiting and supporting candidates and decried the lack of it in their communities.

Others commented that while voters and candidates often divided and could be distinguished on the basis of organized group memberships—social, economic, religious or political—the groups themselves were not active. Another made the following observation: "The groups involved in city elections usually spring from the conduct of the city government in the years immediately preceding the election. If there has been a feeling one section of town has been favored, we find active groups formed in neglected sections to help candidates from those sections. If the city government has tended to become too conservatively business minded, the younger group of citizens tend to organize to help a younger candidate."

TABLE 30

CITIES REPORTING ORGANIZED AND INFORMAL ACTIVITIES

Size of city	Total number of cities	Per cent	
		Both reported	Neither reported
Less than 5,000	53	4	72
5,000- 25,000	94	15	50
25,000- 100,000	38	21	26
100,000 and more	7	57	0
TOTAL	192	15	49

RECAPITULATION

The variety of conditions makes generalization difficult. Clearly indicated, nevertheless, is the frequent absence of any formalized political structure or leadership regularly and continually active at the local level. Neither are there, in many cities, identifiable informal groups that regularly engage in local election politics. This is more true of the smaller cities: in almost 60 per cent of them no permanent group activity was reported. In cities over 25,000, sustained activity is generally found, 80 per cent of these cities reporting the existence of regular informal or formal group participation in election politics.

Political participants in local elections include many groups and individuals differing according to the traditions, conditions, and personalities of each community and changing in time—frequently with amazing rapidity. Still, certain groups and interests are more active and influential than others. Cited by at least one-third of the cities as important are the local newspaper, merchants, service clubs, women's organizations, veterans' groups, lay church groups, and improvement associations.

The recruitment of candidates is equally as varied. Many candidates recruit themselves. Often, incumbents on the council, singly or as a group, select candidates; often this selection is preceded by an appointment to a local advisory board or commission. Also, the urging of friends or of such organizations as lodges, neighborhood clubs, or labor unions leads to recruitment. This informal pattern is carried over into the campaign itself where *ad hoc* and individual political organizations are the rule.

The most frequently reported single body of political influentials is "Main Street." Although not without challenge or internal differences, the economic leadership of the community is most often mentioned as the source of candidates, their recruitment, and their support in local election campaigns. Sharing this important position is the local press, sometimes complementing the "Main Street" influence and sometimes exercising an independent role. Significant in California, the press reportedly assumes special importance in a rapidly growing community in which newcomers look to their local paper for information and guidance.

Political leaders and observers in all cities report difficulties in recruiting able council personnel. This is related to general problems of political participation, of course, but the part-time, non-paid status of local office, the concern over political abuse, and the loss of privacy present particular obstacles.

7

Political Parties in
Nonpartisan Elections

OF THE GROUPS ACTIVE IN LOCAL POLITICS ONLY ONE IS of specific concern in the statutes governing nonpartisan munici-pal elections: the political party. The statutes deny to the party the placement on the ballot of the local candidate's political affiliation. Thus the political party, despite its preferred place at the state or national level, is reduced to the same legal status in the political arena as all other groups in the local community—social, religious, economic, or geographical.

Many of the original nonpartisan advocates, to be sure, hoped that the lack of preferential treatment would lead to complete abandonment of local political activity. Indeed, some urged that the parties be prohibited from playing any role in local politics, a wish destined to founder on constitutional as well as practical grounds. To some extent, the hopes of these early reformers have been realized. Charles Adrian concludes: "With few exceptions, nonpartisan elections have accomplished what they were originally designed to do. They have effectively removed the regular party machinery from involvement in certain kinds of local, judicial, and state elections."[1]

Nevertheless, the political parties may play an influential role in local politics, regardless of the ballot form. In fact, the California evidence would suggest that, even in a strongly nonpartisan environment, the parties and partisan influences remain less exceptional than the generalization cited above implies. As noted earlier, the question of partisan activity in city elections continues to be widely and loudly raised, indicating that the issue is far from dead.

The discussion to follow sets forth the current role of the two major political parties in California city elections. The report constitutes not only a phase of a study of local politics but a brief chapter in the analysis of political parties generally. This latter study has only infrequently in recent years concerned itself with the municipal environment. It has even less often focused on the role of the party in a legally nonpartisan system of elections.

THE SIX CITIES

The complete range of partisan activity in California city politics is revealed in the recent political history of the six cities. Partisanship (the impact of the two major parties) ranged from nonexistence in Maywood to the strongly partisan situation in Berkeley where at times, as one observer noted, everything bore the party label *except* the ballot.

The 5,500 registered voters of Maywood constitute less than 10 per cent of the electorate in the local assembly district in which the city is situated and, of course, an even smaller share of the Congressional, supervisorial, or county population. There is, therefore, little motivation for the leadership or organization of either party in the area to seek out Maywood. Within the city,

---

[1] "A Typology for Nonpartisan Elections," *Western Political Quarterly*, XII (June, 1959), 457.

also, motivation or leadership for any partisan activity are similarly lacking. It would have been surprising to discover that party influences played any role in Maywood's local politics; in fact, none were found.

Chico is a city of the same size as Maywood but outside the metropolitan area and constituting a center for the surrounding countryside. The assembly district in which the city is situated is composed of three counties, and the registered voters of Chico constitute about 15 per cent of the district's electorate. The state Senatorial district is composed solely of Butte County in which Chico is the key city. The Congressional district, one of the largest in the nation, includes nineteen counties. Although of far more influence than Maywood, Chico is not large enough to shape partisan contests. This, along with other factors, has produced a low level of intensity in the city's political life. Until recently there has been little party activity in campaigns for state legislative office, and races have often been uncontested. This lack of partisanship carried over into the city scene. What activity existed of party leaders in city affairs or of civic leaders in party affairs was occasional, and party lines were often crossed in both directions. Although there was evidence that registered Republicans more often served in official city positions, the party label appeared entirely incidental to their role as businessmen and service-club leaders. The only overt partisan activity in recent memory had been that related to the recruitment and campaign of an active Democrat for the council, but even here party motives appeared secondary.

But lack of party activity was not necessarily related to size, as indicated by the fact that a similar pattern appeared to exist in San Leandro and Fresno, cities of approximately 66,000 and 133,000 (1960). While party leaders were sometimes active in city politics and city leaders in party affairs in these communities, there seemed little carry-over from one level to the other. Party affiliation did not appear to be the key to any significant support, and frequent examples could be found of Republicans supporting Democrats for city office, and vice versa. Party organizations played no part in city politics, although members might participate on behalf of friends or associates. In both cities, examples of contests for local office between members of the same party were numerous. Both San Leandro and Fresno were also similar in their strongly Democratic registration and in the fairly even split of their vote in recent state and national contests. As in Chico, although proportionately more Republicans held office than their numbers in the community would have indicated, the party label per se did not appear important as an explanation of this fact.

The situation in Pomona (population 67,000) and Berkeley (population 110,000) was different. In both cities, the economic leaders of the community were the dominant forces in local affairs. Despite exceptions, the correlation in both cities between this group and those active in Republican party politics was high.[2] The party campaign apparatus was also employed occasionally in city elections on behalf of Republican candidates. In both cities, the parties were evenly divided in the number of registered voters,

---

[2] De Grazia describes the relationships he feels exist between "Main Street" and the Republican party in this passage of *The Western Public:* "Republicans have greater chances for victory in the West than the basic constituency of the public admits because the Western public is politically unorganized. Since the parties do not have generally effective party organizations, Republicans gain a strong initial advantage from their 'natural' organization. By natural organization, it is meant that the Republicans number among their supporters by far the greater proportion of the business and professional groups who, without changing their way of life, engage in politics as a matter of course. There is no gentry in America, much less in the West, but the Republicans have a great many individual supporters who belong to real estate organizations, publishers' associations, insurance groups, Rotary, Kiwanis, and other fraternal organizations that function continually, and that, without breaking step with their routine operation, can convert themselves into political organizations. The transformation is often not a conscious one. Indeed it may not even be a transformation at all. But society is like a giant spider web of communication and contacts, and Republicans tend to be stationed at the centers of contacts and communications with the society at large. As spare-time politicians, such contact-controllers and opinion leaders can easily bring to bear upon the political process their strong influences and political leadership. In brief, the normal social structure provides an informal Republican Party organization." De Grazia, *The Western Public: 1952 and Beyond* (1954), pp. 184–185.

Agger and Goldrich make clear, however, that there is no automatic relationship between the Republican-dominated "organizational membership structure" in a community and the "local power structure." In "Boom-town," a city of 16,000 population, "even though Republicans dominated the OMS [organizational membership structure], Democrats were among the top leaders. . . . Democrats participate less than Republicans in the OMS but equally in the power structure, and Democrats are among the top leaders. . . . Where economic dominants do not control the power structure, as they did not in Boomtown, opportunities exist for Democrats to move directly into top leader positions without a long apprenticeship in the Republican-dominated social structure. . . . The efficacy of the national organization of the Republican party on Main Street therefore depends on the partisan complexion of the community power structure, which in turn depends upon relationships among the local power, economic and social structures." Agger and Goldrich, "Community Power Structures and Partisanship," *American Sociological Review,* XXIII (August, 1958), 389–392.

but more than 85 per cent of the elected and appointed city officials were registered Republicans. More Republicans stood for election to local office and, when they did run, had a far greater chance of winning than their Democratic counterparts.

However, there were also important differences. In Pomona the Democratic party was a weak and divided body. Its strength in terms of registrants rested in the older parts of the city, the areas of the poorer homes and of small poultry ranches. Little responsible indigenous leadership was apparent in these neighborhoods. The weakness of the party rested partly, too, in the absence of strong labor organizations. The one recent attempt of the Democratic party leadership to exercise influence in the city had divided the movement, as its adherents had split over what others termed an issue irrelevant to party politics. There was no evidence of exclusion of registered Democrats fom local office, and there were examples to the contrary, but most Democratic registrants did not appear to be in the "stream of things," which minimized their role in the official life of the community.

A different picture was apparent in Berkeley. Unlike many of their fellow Californians, most Berkeley Democrats voted their party. Whereas Pomona, for example, with its registrants almost evenly divided between the two parties had given Eisenhower 66 per cent of its vote and Knight 65 per cent in 1952 and 1954, Berkeley, also evenly divided, had voted only 54 per cent for Eisenhower and 49 per cent for Knight.[3] In contrast to Pomona, there was every evidence of active and strong leadership in Democratic party affairs and of a working organization in the field. Half of the city was represented by a Democratic assemblyman, the result admittedly of "convenient" political boundaries, but an indication of strength nevertheless. Democratic party leadership and apparatus had become heavily engaged in local politics, and certain facets of city politics were partisan in every aspect but the form

[3] This same pattern was characteristic of the 1956 and 1958 elections. Pomona, with a 49 per-cent Democratic registration in 1956 voted only 36 per cent for Stevenson, a difference of 13 per cent. Berkeley, registered 54 per cent Democratic gave Stevenson a 46 per-cent vote, a difference of 8 per cent. In 1958, Pomona, now registered 53 per cent Democratic gave Brown 53 per cent of its vote; Berkeley, registered 54 per cent Democratic voted 59 per cent for Brown. For the state as a whole, registered 60 per cent Democratic (two-party totals), Brown gained 59 per cent of the two-party vote. In short, Berkeley continues to vote more Democratic than its registration would suggest on the basis of the state-wide pattern followed in Pomona.

of the ballot. The mayor from 1947–1955 had been a Democratic candidate for congressional and gubernatorial office.

In Pomona, Republican dominance resulted, at least partly, from the absence of Democratic personnel or leadership. In Berkeley, Republican dominance was the result of victory in a strongly contested and at times highly partisan competition. It is difficult to assess accurately whether the partisan character of much of this recent competition is the beginning of a trend, an isolated phenomenon, or is an outcropping of an aspect of local politics that has hitherto been beneath the surface.

THE STATEWIDE SCENE

How partisan are nonpartisan politics? What do local officials and party leaders think about the role of the party in city elections? These questions were made the object of the state-wide survey. This question was asked: "In any election for *city* or *school* office in your city in the last *four* years, has there been any *public or openly visible activity* on the part of either political organization: county committee, local political clubs, party officials or representative, etc.?" Only eighteen (9 per cent) of the 192 cities indicated the existence of such activity; the larger the city the more frequent was an affirmative reply.

TABLE 31

CITIES REPORTING POLITICAL ORGANIZATIONS ACTIVE
IN CITY OR SCHOOL ELECTIONS

Size of city	Total number of cities	Per cent
Less than 10,000	90	2
10,000-50,000	82	13
50,000 and more	20	25
TOTAL	192	9

Of the eighteen cities, one party or both were reported active in mayoralty campaigns in four cities; in school-board campaigns in seven cities; and in city-council races in sixteen cities. (The relatively low figure for mayoralty races indicates the small number of separately elected mayors in the state.) Democratic activity only was reported in five cities, Republican activity only in three cities, and both parties active in nine cities. (For one city, this phase of the question was not answered.)

Similar results were obtained from the questionnaire distributed to county central-committee chairmen of both political parties. An almost identical question to that quoted above, but including consideration of county office, was asked. In 11 (25 per cent) of the 44 counties from which at least one questionnaire was returned, party organization activity in city, county, or school elections was reported. As did the larger city, the larger counties tended to report such activity more frequently.

TABLE 32

<small>COUNTIES REPORTING POLITICAL ORGANIZATIONS
ACTIVE IN CITY, COUNTY, OR SCHOOL ELECTIONS</small>

Size of county	Total number of counties	Per cent
Less than 25,000	14	14
25,000-100,000	22	18
100,000 and more	8	64
TOTAL	44	25

In one county, the Republicans alone were reported active, in three counties the Democrats only, in four counties both parties, and in three counties this part of the question was not answered. No relationship was apparent between the reported existence of party activity and the relative strength of the party in the county in terms of its percentage of the two-party registration. City, county, and school offices all appeared to command a similar interest, each being mentioned in five or six counties.

Table 33 shows the types of political activities reported in the questionnaires.

TABLE 33

<small>POLITICAL ACTIVITY IN CITIES AND COUNTIES, BY PARTY</small>

Political activity	Republicans active		Democrats active	
	Cities	Counties	Cities	Counties
Public endorsement of candidates	5	1	8	3
Use of party precinct machinery	5	3	6	6
Use of funds or fund raising	6	4	3	3

Table 34 shows the appraisal of party activity in the cities.

TABLE 34

NUMBER OF CITIES REPORTING EFFECT OF PARTY ACTIVITY

Activity	When Republicans only were active	When Democrats only were active	When both parties were active
Helped	3	2	6
Made no difference	0	1	3
Hurt	0	2	0

Individual Party Leader Activity.—A related question, asked of both the city and county respondents, emphasized individual rather than organizational participation: "In contrast with political party organizations, are individual party *leaders* in your city [or "area" in the county-chairman questionnaire]—(county committeemen, party campaign chairmen or club officers, and others influential and active in party affairs) also active in elections for *city* office, either as partisans or nonpartisans?" The results are summarized in table 35.

TABLE 35

PARTY LEADER ACTIVITY IN CITY ELECTIONS
Replies from 192 Cities and 44 Counties
(In Per cent)

Extent of activity	Leading Republicans		Leading Democrats	
	Cities	Counties	Cities	Counties
Many active	12	14	10	11
Some active	31	43	31	27
Few active	22	25	26	34
None active	23	14	22	18
No answer	12	4	11	10
TOTAL	100	100	100	100

County chairmen were also asked to provide information identical to that above but with reference to school and county elections. The data indicate that more party leaders are active in county elections than in either city or school elections and that more Republicans are active than Democrats regardless of the type of election:

TABLE 36

COUNTIES REPORTING "SOME" OR "MANY" PARTY LEADERS ACTIVE
IN LOCAL ELECTIONS
(In Per cent of 44 Counties)

Type of election	Leading Republicans	Leading Democrats
County	70	61
City	57	38
School	34	27

The activity of party leaders in city politics exhibited a marked relationship to population, as reported by the city respondents and shown in table 37:

TABLE 37

CITIES REPORTING "SOME" OR "MANY" REPUBLICAN
LEADERS ACTIVE IN CITY ELECTIONS

Size of city	Total number of cities	Per cent
Less than 5,000	53	36
5,000-25,000	94	46
25,000-100,000	38	53
100,000 and more	7	71
TOTAL	192	43

An almost identical pattern was reported for Democratic leaders. Similarly, party leaders were more often reported active in the larger counties. Combining the report for city, county, and school elections, 61 per cent of the replies from the chairmen in counties with a population of 50,000 or more reported that "some" or "many" leaders were active, while the corresponding figure for chairmen in counties under 50,000 was only 29 per cent; these findings held regardless of the type of election and political party. There was no indication that party leaders were more active in counties in which their party was more strongly registered.

In the few counties in which party organizational activity had been reported a larger proportion of party leaders could have been expected to be reported active. This was not borne out, however.

FREQUENCY WITH WHICH LOCAL OFFICIALS BECOME
CANDIDATES FOR STATE AND NATIONAL OFFICE

Party recruitment of local officials.—Party chairmen throughout the state were asked: "Have you or your predecessor *in the past four years* looked to the ranks of city, county, or school office-holders to seek candidates for state or national office?" Slightly more than half of the 58 chairmen reported that they had looked "often" (15 per cent) or "sometimes" (38 per cent); 43 per cent that they had never done so; and the remaining number did not reply. There was no difference in the pattern of Republican and Democratic replies.

Chairmen from the larger counties tended to report more activity along these lines: 42 per cent of the chairmen in counties under 50,000 and 62 per cent of those from the larger counties replied they had often or sometimes looked to the local ranks. There was no reported relationship between the county's political registration and the degree of recruitment activity; for example, Republican chairmen were no more active in recruiting local officials in strongly Republican counties than their colleagues in weakly registered Republican counties.

A few of the chairmen commented on this question. Representing one point of view, a Democratic chairman who had indicated he "often" looked to the ranks of local officials for prospective candidates wrote: "All candidates should have some local political experience prior to attempting to run for higher office such as Congress and State office." However, the opposite view was expressed by a neighboring chairman, also a Democrat:

> Candidates for local offices who have strong partisan backgrounds can seldom hope to be elected except in extraordinary circumstances. Therefore, if you accept the premise that the bulk of these officials have weak partisan backgrounds it generally follows that the majority of them are not too acceptable to party leaders as candidates for partisan offices. Also, local officials are directly on the firing line and seldom have their meetings attended by anyone except those people who are angry about something or violently against some proposal. They make many enemies

and few friends. They are not detached from their constituents such as state legislators or federal legislators are.

A Republican chairman concurred, but for a different reason: "Local officials often do a good deal of fence-riding during their term of office and therefore are unacceptable to either political party as good representatives." The extent to which these opposing views have been followed is suggested below.

Local officials who seek partisan office.—Both city and county respondents were asked: "In the last ten years, as best as you can remember, has any local official (city, county, or school) or ex-local official actually run for state or national office in your area?" [4] The evidence from both this source of information and that described below suggests that persons who have held local elective office frequently also compete at the state or national level. Respondents from 29 per cent of the 192 cities reported that a total of 74 local officials had stood for higher office in their area "in the last ten years." In 29 of the 44 counties, a total of 47 local officials were similarly reported. Many of these, of course, may have been the same persons referred to by city respondents in the same area.

The tendency was more pronounced in the larger cities.

TABLE 38

CITIES REPORTING LOCAL OFFICIALS HAVING RUN
FOR STATE OR NATIONAL OFFICE

Size of city	Total number of cities	Per cent
Less than 10,000	90	11
10,000-100,000	95	43
100,000 and more	7	71
TOTAL	192	29

Similarly, 8 of the 19 counties having a population of less than 50,000 and 21 of the 25 larger counties reported that some local official had stood for higher office. These data may indicate

---

[4] This question placed heavy emphasis upon the memory of the respondent, and the answers cannot be regarded as representing more than a broad approximation of the facts. Secondly, there may have been duplication in the data; for example, two replies from adjoining cities might have referred to the same county official.

nothing more than the obvious fact that in larger cities and counties there are more local officials and state or national offices to be filled.

The various combinations of local office held and partisan office sought, with an indication of whether the candidate was successful, are indicated in table 39.

TABLE 39

NUMBER OF LOCAL OFFICEHOLDERS WHO SOUGHT STATE OR
NATIONAL OFFICE, 1945-1955

Office held	Office sought	Reported by county respondents		Reported by city respondents	
		Number of candidates		Number of candidat s	
		Entered	Successful	Entered	Successful
Mayor	Congress	*4*	*1*	*3*	*1*
	State Senate	*2*	*2*	*6*	*3*
	Assembly	*4*	*4*	*12*	*8*
		10	7	21	12
Councilman	Congress	*1*	*0*	*9*	*1*
	State Senate	*0*	*0*	*2*	*0*
	Assembly	*7*	*3*	*18*	*7*
		8	3	29	8
Supervisor	Congress	*4*	*0*	*4*	*0*
	State Senate	*10*	*2*	*4*	*2*
	Assembly	*4*	*1*	*3*	*3*
		18	3	11	5
District attorney	State Senate	2	2	2	2
Miscellaneous	Miscellaneous	9	4	11	3
TOTAL		47	19	74	30
Per cent successful		—	40	—	41

Allowing for the fact that table 39 undoubtedly contains duplications, the data lead to the not surprising generalization that the higher the local office held and the lower the level of the partisan post sought, the better appear the chances for success.

PREVIOUS LOCAL-GOVERNMENT EXPERIENCE OF STATE AND NATIONAL OFFICIALS

Using the published biographies of the state's elected partisan officials as a source it can be ascertained how many of them held local-government posts before assuming state or national office.[5]

TABLE 40

LOCAL-GOVERNMENT EXPERIENCE OF ELECTED CALIFORNIA STATE AND NATIONAL OFFICIALS

Elected state or national officials		Elected state or national officials who previously held a local office[a]							
Office	Number	Mayor[b]	Council-man	Super-visor	School trustee	District attorney	Judge	Advisory committee	Misc.
1960									
State-wide[c]	10	1	1	0	2	1	1	2	0
Congress	32	2	2	1	2	1	1	2	0
State Senate	40	0	2	2	2	4	4	2	2
Assembly	80	10	2	2	4	0	1	10	2
TOTAL[d]	162	13	7	5	10	6	7	16	4
1954									
State-wide	10	0	3	0	1	1	1	2	0
Congress	32	2	2	1	1	1	0	2	1
State Senate	40	3	1	4	5	5	3	1	1
Assembly	80	6	5	1	3	0	4	6	0
TOTAL[e]	162	11	11	6	10	7	8	11	2
1950									
State-wide	10	0	3	0	1	2	1	1	0
Congress	25	2	2	1	1	1	0	1	1
State Senate	40	4	2	2	6	5	3	1	0
Assembly	80	3	5	0	3	1	1	7	2
TOTAL[f]	155	9	12	3	11	9	5	10	3
1942									
State-wide	10	0	3	0	0	1	0	0	0
Congress	22	0	3	2	0	1	0	0	0
State Senate	40	2	2	3	3	1	3	0	1
Assembly	80	5	2	0	6	1	0	1	1
TOTAL[g]	152	7	10	5	9	4	3	1	2

a One official may be listed under several categories depending on number of local offices held.
b Mayors appointed from the council are included only in the mayor's column.
c "State-wide" includes governor, lieutenant-governor, attorney-general, secretary of state, state controller, treasurer, and board of equalization members. (The last-mentioned are elected from districts.)
d In 1960, 52 state and national officials had held local office, including 41 in an elective post.
e In 1954, 53 state and national officials had held local office, including 46 in an elective post.
f In 1950, 50 state and national officials had held local office, including 44 in an elective post.
g In 1942, 37 state and national officials had held local office, including 35 in an elective post.
SOURCE: State of California, *California Blue Book 1954, 1950,* and *1942* (Sacramento: State Printing Office); Floyd and Agnes Booe, *Members of the California Legislature and Other State Officials* (undated, but including officeholders following 1958 election).

[5] State and national officials also occasionally seek local office, of course, particularly in the larger cities. The Los Angeles city council, for example, includes several former state assemblymen; the mayor of that city was previously in Congress.

Following the 1958 election, for example, 52 or almost one-third of the 162 elected state and national officials had held some local office; these included 41 or 25 per cent who had run for and been successful in elected city, county, school, or judicial office.

It is often asserted that one reason for the past preponderance of Republican office holders at the state and national level in California is the fact that Republican members dominate local office and are recruited or advance themselves into the higher posts. It is true that Republicans hold more than their proportionate share of nonpartisan offices. But answers are not available to the questions of whether local officials fare better when they run for higher office than do those who have not held local office and whether more Republicans than Democrats with local-government experience actually stand for higher office. It is clear that the proportion of Democrats in state or national office as of 1960 who had held local elective office was considerably larger (31 per cent) than the proportion of Republicans (16 per cent). A cause-effect relationship between Republican dominance of local offices and subsequent Republican success in state and national elections cannot be readily assumed.

The Attitude of Respondents Concerning a Partisan Form of Local Ballot.— The last question asked of city and county respondents was: "Finally, if you would care to give your opinion, would you favor a state or city law requiring that the political affiliation, if any, of candidates for *city* office be entered on the city election ballot following the candidate's name?" The replies were:

TABLE 41

ATTITUDES OF RESPONDENTS TOWARD DESIRABILITY OF A PARTISAN CITY BALLOT
(In Number of Respondents)

	Editors or publishers	Mayors	City managers	City clerks	Miscellaneous	County chairmen	
						Republicans	Democrats
Yes	4	3	3	0	0	1	18
Depends	1	0	1	0	0	0	0
No	40	93	84	18	11	27	11
Don't know	0	0	0	0	0	0	0
No answer	1	4	1	1	0	0	1
TOTAL	46	100	89	19	11	28	30

Of the various groups of respondents, only the Democratic

county central-committee chairmen favored a change in the ballot form. Of the seven persons who answered "yes" or "depends" among the mayors and city managers, five were registered Democrats, one was a Republican, and one not ascertained.

In a 1959 survey, conducted independently, 38 party chairmen responded to a written questionnaire that asked: "Would you favor partisan election of supervisors, councilmen and mayors?" The replies are shown in table 42:[6]

TABLE 42

ATTITUDE OF PARTY CHAIRMEN TOWARD PARTISAN LOCAL ELECTIONS

Attitude	Republican county chairmen		Democratic county chairmen	
	Number	Per cent	Number	Per cent
Yes	7	35	11	61
No	13	65	7	39
TOTAL	20	100	18	100

The wording of the two questions is not identical, but they are similar enough to make a comparison of the 1955 and 1959 surveys appropriate. No sign of a change in attitude among Democratic county chairmen is indicated, although the two samples included only four Democratic chairmen who had participated in both surveys. Sixty per cent favored a partisan ballot in 1955 and 61 per cent in 1959. Among the Republicans, only one of the 28 chairmen supported a partisan ballot in 1955, but one-third of the 20 chairmen did so in 1959. However, none of the four Republicans participating in both surveys changed their position. Therefore, the more favorable attitude toward local partisanship among Republican chairmen reflects the opinions of new or different chairmen, not a switch in individual attitudes. The evidence is clearly too limited to suggest a shift in the Republican position on this issue.

The question of a partisan ballot provoked frequent written comment among both city and county participants in the statewide survey. Several city respondents observed that party politics had no relevance to local affairs, particularly in the small city. As one city manager from a community of 5,000 put it: "Party affiliation merely gives the individual a place to hang his hat going in the

[6] Angelo, "Party Reorganization and Election Reform in California" (1959), pp. 82–83.

voting booth." A mayor from a city of the same size observed: "The average middle class citizen carries far more weight and influence and will work harder for what they think is right than any other class, and political parties don't mean a thing to the majority of them."

Some expressed concern that a partisan ballot would make it difficult for those registered with the minority party in the particular city to gain office and would discourage them from running. One mayor in a very small city stated:

> We happen to be located in a heavy Democratic area and might lose the use of many good Republicans, who because of their political party might lose the necessary few votes for election. It is hard enough to get good men to give up their time and take the abuse.

The mayor was apparently not aware that the city was evenly split in its registration between the two parties. A fellow mayor in a city of 7,000 where registered Republicans were clearly in the majority (60 per cent) made a similar statement:

> I am very much against party politics in city elections. It is the purest form of government today on the whole, and this is due to not being complicated by party considerations. ——— is 75 per cent Republican in the last general election and yet at times four of the five councilmen have been Democrats. [One out of the five was so registered at the time the statement was made.]

A city manager from a town of 12,000 made a different observation in voicing criticism of the partisan ballot: "Locally, a man's political affairs are considered his own. Municipal elections are strictly for the man. Party people as such would not win a local election."

Other communities reported that political parties of one or both camps had been informally active and that the results had generally been favorable. In several instances, examples were cited of local officials who were also official party officers, such as county chairmen or committeemen. These comments did not, of course, necessarily imply that the respondent favored a partisan ballot at the local level, and in fact the opposite view was sometimes suggested. For example, in a small town of 5,000, it was noted that the local Republican Assembly group have, not as a group, but as members (using precinct methods) supported candidates. However, they have supported two Democrats as well as Republican candidates, and in fact backed a Democrat over a Republican for the city council. They supported the man.

In another city of 20,000 the respondent discussed the Good Government Committee, formed at election time by Democratic activists to sponsor a team of candidates. He noted that while most of the candidates had been excellent men,

> the voters have been reluctant to vote all of them in at any one time. Perhaps this reluctance has been of "machine" politics or it has been due to the personality of the candidates. At times it appears the group has wanted to be the power behind the throne—guiding and grooming individuals for higher political office. At other times it appeared they wanted to gain some particular concession. In my opinion, there is nothing wrong in their efforts since they do no more than other loosely knit groups, formed at election times. The main difference is they are well organized, and I would not like to see any such organization gain control because regardless of their present motive, groups have in some instances charted a course to benefit their organization more than the city they were elected to serve.

The case *for* party activity, as viewed by one city manager, was expressed in these words: "Effective local government depends on organized political action by organized groups. Party organization may not be the best, but it is better than no organization."

Comments on both sides were made by the county central-committee chairmen; more than three times as many written comments came from Democratic chairmen as from their Republican counterparts. Typical of one viewpoint was this statement from a Republican chairman:

> In a rural area such as ours there has been no strong partisanship even in partisan offices such as State Senator and Assemblyman. The population of the county (70,000) is such that candidates for any office are still considered on an individual merit basis rather than a political basis. This may change as the population increases; time will tell.

A Democratic chairman in a small county (20,000) stated:

> In general, in city, county, and school elections there ap-
> pears no connection with the national parties. I do not feel
> that the lack of partisanship results from lack of interest; I
> think that the residents of this county keep as well informed
> as the state average, perhaps a notch or two better.

Another Democrat did not comment on the desirability of a partisan ballot but noted:

> If and when we do have a candidate in a future election
> we will probably back him as "The Committee for so and
> so." That is not give him official Democratic support—in the
> open at least. This is not my idea, but the opinion of a
> majority of our active local Democrats. They believe that
> in a rural community such as ——— (20,000 pop.), the
> stigma of the party label would be injurious. There is some
> validity to this opinion. With city elections independent of
> the general elections the candidate on a city election ticket
> carrying open party support does not have the advantage
> and impetus of a strong state or federal candidate running
> on the same ticket.

On one occasion, the chairman referred the question to a larger
group:

> Question 5 was submitted to the Executive Committee of
> the ——— Democratic Club, a two-county organization, and
> they were unanimously agreed that in an area where the
> population is not as heavy as in the larger cities [combined
> population of the counties was 60,000], politics should be
> kept on a nonpartisan basis, as both parties seek a common
> goal.

However, a plea for the nonpartisan system also came from a
Democratic chairman in one of the state's larger counties
(350,000):

> I feel that the issues that involve city government have
> practically no connection with the policies of the two major
> parties. Party denomination would only confuse the issues
> and, in some areas, make it impossible for men that are
> willing to give their time for nothing to serve on city coun-
> cils, e.g., ——— is a predominately Republican city which
> consistently gives large majorities to Republican candidates

in partisan elections—yet 4 out of 5 city councilmen are
registered Democrats. The city of ––– has the exact same
situation. Therefore partisan backing would be a kiss of
death to many able city councilmen.

Two Democratic chairmen raised the separate matter of the
practicality of party activity in local affairs; one stated:

Our party has been too fully occupied on the state and
national level to be adequately concerned with local elections—if a sound Democratic candidate offered himself we
would support him, but we haven't sought for any such
candidate.

The other chairman observed:

I would hesitate to add this to the existing problems of
party activity although the present system presents difficulties in organization which do not exist in those areas
having local partisan elections.

Viewpoints concerning the existence or advisability of partisan
activity in local politics were expressed almost entirely by Democratic chairmen. The statements suggested: that local nonpartisan
government is Republican; that party philosophy is also pertinent
at the local level; and that organized party activity might help
spotlight vice and corruption.

The first point was expressed by the Democratic chairmen of a
small county (45,000):

As in other counties, the Republicans are successful here in
the Court House aided, of course, by the press and the
Chamber of Commerce. The latter, in my opinion, is an unofficial wing of the Republican Party.

From a colleague in a larger county (100,000) came this observation:

Republicans who run for nonpartisan offices seem to collect
the support of Republican powers better than do the Democrats. This later produces trouble for Democrats in seeking
candidates for partisan offices.

Another small county chairman (20,000) felt that

candidates for city and county office are predominantly Republicans because they come from the group who can af-

ford to hold office with a nominal salary, always either
businessmen or ranchers. . . . If political affiliation were
required the offices would be filled by Democrats and
salaries raised to compensate for ability.

In this county at the time of the questionnaire four of nine elected
county officials were Democrats and four of the five elected city
officials in the one city of the county were so registered. The
chairman was apparently unaware of his own party's strength!

The second viewpoint was expressed by a Democratic chairman in a large county (425,000):

I basically believe in partisan offices throughout our government system, as I feel the handling of local government is
just as much one of political philosophy as in state or
national government.

More to the point was the expression of a Democratic chairman in
a county of 175,000 who stated, "I want to know the political
thinking of the 'dog catcher.'"

The last expressions of attitude came from two Democratic
chairmen in large counties (250,000) with strong vice problems.
Said one:

In the absence of party activity, whatever division there is
probably lies between those who want strict enforcement of
the law and those who prefer not-so-strict enforcement. This
issue is not openly dealt with and is, of course, not a healthy
one. Probably some sort of group responsibility would tend
to bring this out in the open and thereby limit it.

The other respondent, not necessarily focusing on vice commented:

I am convinced party participation in city, county and school
elections will forestall future political corruption which is
evident only to those at the present time who are in close
contact with political conditions. We have only one newspaper and it is Republican. Exposure is difficult. But party
activity in all elective offices would cast the light of publicity
on all elective offices. Therefore, I favor political affiliation
of all elective offices.

Key ology

RECAPITULATION

Political parties and partisanship are not irrelevant in nonpartisan politics. In California, party influence varies widely from city to city—from unimportance to a major force shaping local political life.

Formal activity by the two party organizations is relatively infrequent in local politics. Only one-quarter of the cities with a population of more than 50,000 reported "public or openly visible activity," and the percentage of such cities declined still further among the smaller communities. However, nearly half of all cities indicated that at least some party leaders are active in local nonpartisan politics. Here, too, such activity is more pronounced in large cities, three-quarters of the cities of 100,000 or more reporting participation of political leaders.

Many of these persons take part in local politics as community leaders rather than as party officials; their motives are often nonpartisan as evidenced by their support of local candidates of the opposite party. On the other hand, partisan considerations may often intrude. One reason for this is that many county chairmen look to the city hall and court house as sources of candidates for state or national office. Nonpartisan officeholders frequently compete for partisan office, and many are successful. In 1960, 52 of California's 162 elected state or federal officials previously held local office, either elected or appointed. The 51 included a larger than proportionate share of Democrats, a fact which qualifies the hypothesis that past Republican successes were based on G.O.P dominance of local politics.

Most local officials and most Republican county chairmen wish to continue nonpartisan elections. Sixty per cent of the Democratic chairmen, on the other hand, favor a partisan ballot. The arguments advanced by California local and party officials in favor of nonpartisan elections are: Members of the minority party can participate more freely and effectively; local politics are based on personality considerations, particularly in small communities; local issues have no connection with major party platforms, and party designation would confuse the issues; parties are fully occu-

pied with state and national politics. Partisan advocates, on the
other hand, put forth these views: Party activity is better than no
activity, which too often exists; Republicans have a dispropor-
tionate influence in nonpartisan politics; local government is influenced just as much by policy and philosophical differences as
state and national government; partisanship would lead to group
responsibility which would forestall corruption and bring public
issues more into the limelight.

8

The Politics of Acquaintance and Personalities

THE GROUPS AND PERSONS DISCUSSED IN PRECEDING CHAP-
ters participate in local campaigns in many ways and for many
reasons. Some merely make small campaign contributions. Others
do little more than give a public endorsement with the hope that
the indication of support in the press or an advertisement will influence others to vote for the endorsed candidate. Others make a
personal effort on behalf of the candidate, either in word-of-
mouth campaigning among their friends or in actual campaign
activity. Most citizens, of course, do not take part in the campaign, and for many it has little meaning. More than half of the

registered voters generally fail to vote in a municipal race.[1] Nevertheless, the election campaign is of key importance in shaping the character of local politics. It may more often influence the election outcome than would be true of state or national races, which are more likely to be affected by national or world events and trends beyond the reach of the immediate campaign.

The Politics of Acquaintance.—Particularly important in the local election is "the politics of acquaintance," that is, the informal word-of-mouth politicking between friends and associates that occurs at such places as the service-club luncheon, the legion hall, the women's book club, the union headquarters, the lodge, the chamber of commerce, the charity organization. It is a form of politics not generally identifiable as such. Rather, it is the by-product of a highly organized community in which these groups provide the principal avenues of the day-to-day communication and contact pertinent to city politics. Usually, such activity is no more than a conversation between friends concerning their choice on election day. The cumulative effect of these informal discussions, repeated by the hundreds, however, looms as one of the most important aspects of any local campaign, particularly in small to medium-sized cities. This is true not only in influencing the choice of a particular candidate but also in stimulating a person to go to the polls.

To be sure, the "politics of acquaintance" is a feature of every political campaign. Even at the presidential level, face-to-face relationships between a potential voter and a partisan friend have their impact. This relationship probably is more important as one descends the political ladder, as national trends lessen in importance and more parochial considerations increase, but this hypothesis was not tested in this study. It is clear, however, that this activity is at times the paramount, if not the sole, characteristic of local campaigns, and that in every city, regardless of size, an awareness of this phenomenon is essential to an understanding of community politics. This may be particularly true in an election system free, formally at least, from the more organized structure and activity implied by the partisan ballot.

---

[1] In the six cities, the turnout in municipal elections, based on the percentage of those registered to vote for the nearest general state election, ranged from 29 to 48 per cent. See page 136.

For example, 2,000 votes would win any council election in Chico; a vote as low as 1,100, in a race with many candidates and with plurality victories permitted, has been sufficient to gain office in recent years. In the absence of controversy over civic issues—and such controversy has generally been absent from Chico election campaigns in recent years—these votes are gained primarily through personal acquaintance, either with the candidate or with someone who knows him. And knowledge of the candidate is obtained primarily through the organized groups.

A popular and active Mason in Chico, for example, is probably known personally or by name to a majority of the 500–700 Masons, most of whom also have voting members in their families. A solid vote of this group alone, based not on the fact that the candidate is a Mason, but that he is identifiable by name and well regarded, would nearly bring election success. If a typical candidate, however, he would also belong to the Elks, the Rotary Club, the chamber of commerce, and to one of Chico's many active churches, each group including some persons not members of the other groups and bringing the candidate within striking range of 2,000 votes, solely on the basis of the memberships and family relations of the few organizations to which he personally belongs. To this, of course, must be added the "unearned increment" of votes which any candidate obtains merely because his name appears on the ballot.

The "politics" here described does not comprise formal participation of these groups in the local campaign, their endorsement of a candidate, or other overt activity. Rather, in the conduct of their normal day-to-day routine these groups serve as vehicles for political activity in the community. To emphasize campaign activity per se in a community heavily influenced by the "politics of acquaintance" is to substitute appearance for reality.

These avenues of internal communication are not in equal measure available to all groups or candidates in a community. Those to whom they are readily accessible can frequently turn informal activity into a formal political mechanism. For example, the ladies aid society, although not publicly identified, can become an arm of the political campaign of the favored candidate or slate as meaningfully as though it were a regular political organ.

The business community, broadly defined, has these resources of internal communication to a greater measure than other segments of the population for reasons suggested in chapter vi. The net effect is to provide "Main Street" with natural political advantages not possessed by other groups, at least not to the same degree.

THE POLITICS OF GROUP MOBILIZATION

In most local election campaigns, the politics of acquaintance is accompanied by what might be termed the politics of group mobilization. Particularly in the larger communities, reliance is placed less on personal contact and face-to-face relationships than on the more formal and indirect communication typically associated with a political campaign.

Unlike the "typical" campaign, however, the local nonpartisan contest is conducted in an informal, fluid, and *ad hoc* atmosphere, in which such terms as "the machine," "the boss," and the more traditional language used in descriptions of local politics are misleading or irrelevant. Regular organized activity on the local scene is more often absent than present in California city election politics.

This general lack of permanent formal activity is evidenced in the campaign itself. In the six cities, for example, paper organizations were occasionally established to back a candidate or a slate under some such title as Good Government League for Smith, but no formal group was openly active in the local campaign, except, sometimes, women's groups and labor unions. In these latter instances, the interest of the organizations was almost entirely focused on some one candidate, a woman or a union official, and noticeably unconcerned with more general issues or programs. At times, of course, other groups in the community are "unofficially" active in a similar fashion. The informal work of the improvement associations in one city, the "downtown group" in a second, and the Democratic party in a third, for example, appear to have been clearly identified in the public mind.

More typical of the local elections surveyed, however, is the development of *ad hoc* support, organization, and funds by the individual candidate. Rather than being recruited by a group and assuming its apparatus, the average candidate develops his own campaign from the ground up.

Successful election politics depends on the mobilization and activation behind the candidate or slate of the right combination of many groups and persons, differing according to community and changing in time. Never can there be complete assurance that the right combination will influence a majority of the voters, although at times predictability is high. In some communities, the approval of one group will almost certainly bring the support of others. Elsewhere, however, no such implied hierarchy exists, and each community segment must be won independently.[2]

This type of politics is distinguished from that of a regular partisan campaign for a state or national candidate by the *relative* flexibility that features the local campaign. Freed from overt party identification and loyalty and a panoply of state and national issues, groups and individuals form and reform, become active and inactive, and switch candidate loyalties far more readily than is observable in partisan state or national campaigns, even in California! In such an unstructured pattern of politics, the type and intensity of the more formal campaign activities vary, as one might expect, between the six cities and, also, within the cities, between elections.

Common to all municipal campaigns is the use of newspaper advertisements. Sometimes these are merely announcements of an incumbent who is practically assured of reëlection, indicating as a courteous gesture that he is not taking the public for granted. Sometimes, advertising is reported to be the key to more favorable editorial or news coverage, but one suspects (and hopes) this practice is confined to only a few of the smallest papers. Often, newspaper advertising is the principal method of campaigning, in which opposing candidates state their qualifications and their views on public issues.

Similarly, almost every candidate in the six cities appeared at one or more "meet the candidates" nights sponsored by a local organization, although the importance of such appearances seems limited. All candidates, too, generally sought to attend a round of

---

[2] Wood describes much the same pattern: "In place of the outright politician, the professional who works full time at his job, residents look to 'wheels' to spark civic affairs—men and women who engage in politics as their avocation, and occasionally as their recreation. Sometimes regarded as conscientious citizens, sometimes as simply incurable extroverts finding release for their energies, the amateur dabblers in public affairs shape local policy. The pattern of politics which emerges from their efforts often provokes intricate maneuverings among competing groups, lively conflict and sharp disagreements; and it is volatile and complex." Wood, *Suburbia: Its People and Their Politics* (1958), p. 175.

service-club luncheons, lodge meetings, and the like. Rarely are political speeches made at such occasions; rather, the candidate is introduced by some friendly member to his colleagues with the statement that the guest is a candidate for the city council. This, of course, is a variant of the "politics of acquaintance" discussed above.

A wide range of paid publicity in addition to newspaper advertising is used in local campaigns, from pocket cards to television programs and including bumper strips, posters, quarter cards, postcard and leaflet mailings, brochures for distribution, and radio and TV spots. The general absence of publicity devices in the small city of Chico was noteworthy. However, in Maywood, a city of the same population as Chico (15,000), campaigning by newspaper advertising and mailed or distributed leaflets was the general practice. The impersonal character of metropolitan Maywood compared to the close-knit Chico environment suggests a reason for the difference. Of the six cities, Fresno made the most intensive use of paid publicity. This is attributable to at least three factors: (1) Fresno elections are especially competitive and the elections have featured many candidates; (2) until 1958, three of the positions were full-time and paid;[3] (3) candidates have a greater incentive to use expensive campaign media—newspaper, radio, and TV—when, as in Fresno, the central city of a large farming area, these media serve primarily the local audience and are not dissipated throughout a number of other cities in metropolitan areas.

Campaigns in the other larger cities corresponded to those of Fresno in the devices employed, but not in quantity. Some use of radio was reported in Berkeley and Pomona, although it is not a very efficient medium for most cities in metropolitan areas; more emphasis was placed on printed literature. In Berkeley, especially, it was clear that the burden of campaigning generally fell on the contenders, not the incumbents, many of whom campaigned hardly at all; a public pamphlet in Berkeley, sent to each voter and containing the photograph, background, and platform of every candidate, reduced the need for well-known incumbents to advertise.

---

[3] Fresno was the last California city to employ the commission form of government. A council-administrative officer charter was approved by the voters and became effective in the spring of 1958.

In the four larger cities, professional advertising or public-relations firms had been employed on occasion, but were not regarded as essential. Nor did these firms, generally speaking, play a more important role than designing publicity materials. It was not reported that a public-relations organization or individual had assumed responsibility for leadership of the campaign, as in some state elections in California. This practice is probably confined to the largest cities and the most expensive campaigns.

There are, of course, means of campaigning other than the paid devices described. One of the more popular is the coffee hour, conducted in the homes of supporters of the candidate living in particular neighborhoods throughout the city; another is the telephone canvass. Both activities are usually conducted by housewives. Only in Berkeley, and related to the activities of certain Democratic party workers, was widespread precinct canvassing reported. This phase of campaigning requires more manpower and a higher degree of organization than most California cities command, even in state or national races.

THE COST OF LOCAL ELECTION CAMPAIGNS

The amount of money necessary to campaign for local office, is a frequent but highly elusive subject of political research. Official reports of contributions or expenditures, only recently required in California at the local level, are far from satisfactory. In the state-wide survey, this question was asked: "Would you estimate the range of cost of a typical successful campaign for council?" The replies, as shown in table 43 indicate, as might be expected, that the larger the city the greater the cost.[4] However, the range of costs reported from communities of the same general population classification is indicative of the variety of political conditions in California cities. Such factors as the intensity and tradition of local competition, the type of media available and used in the campaign, and the existence of active and organized groups, all appear to have a relation to costs, independent of the number of voters.

---

[4] There were a few elections, apparently, when the amounts indicated related to a slate campaign, rather than an individual campaign. The costs were recorded as reported, however.

TABLE 43

Cost of Successful City Council Campaign

Size of city	Number of cities reporting	$0-99	$100-249	$250-499	$500-999	$1,000-2,499	$2,500-4,999	$5,000-7,499	$7,500-9,999
		Per cent of cities reporting							
0-4,999	42	93	5	2	0	0	0	0	0
5,000-9,999	30	63	27	10	0	0	0	0	0
10,000-24,999	52	27	37	17	12	6	1	0	0
25,000-49,999	20	0	20	25	30	25	0	0	0
50,000-99,999	10	0	10	40	20	20	10	0	0
100,000-249,999	4	0	0	0	25	25	50	0	0
250,000-499,999	1	0	0	0	0	0	0	0	100
500,000-999,999	0	0	0	0	0	0	0	0	0
1,000,000 and more	1	0	0	0	0	0	0	0	100
TOTAL	160	45	21	14	9	7	3	0	1

A similar question was asked about the cost of a typical successful mayor's campaign, in those cities in which the mayor is separately elected. Respondents from fourteen such cities answered this question. Again, there is a relationship between the size of city and the cost of the campaign, as is indicated by table 44. The one city in the 250,000–500,000 population class estimated a range of costs from $10,000 to $25,000, while the estimates for

TABLE 44

Cost of Successful Campaign for Mayor

Size of city	Number of cities reporting	Median cost in dollars
10,000-25,000	5	100-249
25,000-50,000	3	1,000-2,499
50,000-100,000	4	1,000-2,499
250,000 and more	2	10,000 and more

a Los Angeles mayor's campaign ranged from $30,000 to $100,000.

The range of campaign expenditures in the six cities was reported as shown in table 45. These costs are generally consistent, in relation to size of city, with those reported for the cities of the state as a whole.

All six cities reported that there was little "big money" con-

TABLE 45

CAMPAIGN EXPENDITURES IN SIX CITIES

(In Dollars)

City	Mayoralty race	Commission or council race
Fresno	5,000-10,000	800-3,000
Berkeley	2,000-3,000	50-3,000
Pomona	800-2,200	30-500
San Leandro	—	500-2,000
Maywood	—	50-500
Chico	—	300-500

tributed to local campaigns. Instead, the treasury for the individual candidate or slate appears to be filled by a number of small contributions, rarely exceeding $100; the candidate himself may be the chief contributor to his campaign. Organization contributions from local interests, such as utilities, contractors, and railroads, were occasionally reported but rarely as large amounts. Two possible exceptions may be noted: Labor-union support in Fresno and Berkeley may be significant in union-officials' campaigns. Secondly, large sums of gambling money were probably poured into recent Fresno mayoralty campaigns in an effort to make Fresno again an open city. It remains to be seen whether Democratic party money will continue to be regularly diverted into local Berkeley campaigns as it has been in recent elections.

THE EXTENT OF CANDIDATE SLATES

Respondents to the state-wide questionnaire were asked: "Do candidates generally run as individuals, as part of a slate, or do they do both?" The replies were distributed as indicated in table 46. Slate activity (including cities which indicated "both") was

TABLE 46

FREQUENCY OF INDIVIDUAL VERSUS SLATE CAMPAIGNS

(In Per cent of 192 Cities)

Type of campaign	Per cent of cities
Individual	64
Slate	5
Both	28
Don't know	3

reported by respondents from 23 to 56 per cent of the cities in the various population categories, with the exception of the two cities of more than 250,000 from which only individual activity was reported; this last fact is not surprising because in Los Angeles candidates are elected from districts and in San Diego they are nominated from districts and elected at large. As might be expected slate activity was reported least frequently in cities under 5,000—23 per cent, as contrasted with 65 per cent of the cities in the 25,000–50,000 category.

Of the six cities, only San Leandro and Maywood had a record of formal candidate slates, based on local personality and factional considerations. In the other four cities related but informal activity occurred. For example, recent Berkeley campaigns have seen, particularly among Democratic candidates, frequent evidences of joint campaigning, but rarely publicly identified as such. Similar activities were occasionally observed in Pomona and Chico. More typical, however, was the Fresno pattern of a series of individual campaigns, separately identified, organized, administered, and financed.

ISSUES AND PERSONALITIES AS FACTORS
IN LOCAL CAMPAIGNS

Local elections more often center on personalities than issues.[5] Community consensus on the questions facing the city is frequently so general that the only serious problem of candidate choice centers not on "what does he stand for," but "what are his qualifications." This observation is not peculiar to local government. It is frequently said about national elections that a new administration will not change policies, but merely those who administer them, and a common complaint hurled at the "outs" is that all they promise is "to do the same thing better." [6] The stress

---

[5] This characteristic is not restricted to nonpartisan elections in the United States, Birch, writing about an English town of 20,000, states that "in municipal elections the party labels count less than the personalities of the candidates and the extent to which they are known by the electors." *Small Town Politics: A Study of Political Life in Glossop* (1959), p. 114.

[6] With a somewhat broader emphasis than is here presented, Gouldner suggests the relative influence of local personalities: "During the last century, American political leadership has undergone vast and sweeping changes. Among many changes, the decline in personalized forms of persuasion and leadership

on personality considerations was clearly indicated by the replies from the 192 cities to the question: "In the last election campaigns for mayor and/or council, have the races been decided more on the basis of issues or on the basis of personalities?" Three-fourths of the respondents replied "personalities." One-eighth replied "issues" and the remaining eighth "both"—between them constituting 13 per cent of cities under 5,000 and 30 per cent of cities between 5,000 and 250,000.[7]

Respondents indicated specific issues in the local campaigns. Taxes, economy, or city fiscal policy were mentioned in 9 cities. In 8 cities, the issues were cited in such general terms as community progress, good government, level of services, or the manner in which the city is run. The council-manager form of government

---

seems one of the most crucial. . . . These changes find their expression primarily in the national and state political arenas. For the present . . . political relationships in the neighborhood and local communities remain highly personalized." Gouldner, ed., *Studies in Leadership* (1950), p. 303.

Providing some explanation for this shift, two commentators concluded as follows upon completion of a study of a small New England city: "The growth of state and national governmental powers and the accompanying increasing regulation of economic activities, shifted attention to the state and national political scenes. With stability, the local political issues at the same time became smaller in scope. Bay City's local problems were mainly those of maintenance and replacement rather than of extension of municipal facilities and services. . . . With the disappearance of 'bread-and-butter' issues from the local scene and the rise of the political power of the newer ethnic groups, local issues centered more around style than economics. Who shall control the city government became more important than what the city government shall do." Alice S. and Peter H. Rossi, "An Historical Perspective on the Functions of Local Politics," unpublished paper presented at the 1956 meeting of the American Sociological Society, p. 10.

---

[7] The determination of whether issues or candidates are more important in influencing the outcome of the local election cannot finally be resolved by this investigation. In *The Voter Decides* (1954), Campbell, Gurin, and Miller proposed that voter motivation might be considered in terms of party identification, candidate orientation, and issue orientation but stressed their belief that "no single-factor theory will account for voting behavior" (p. 87). Their analysis was based on comprehensive national polling and had reference to the 1952 presidential election.

This study of local politics did not include any public opinion polling, and the evidence is not sufficient to suggest the relevance of the findings reported in the text to those of the 1952 presidential study. However, the three factors of candidate, issue, and party take on different characteristics in local politics. Candidate orientation has a different meaning when the orientation is, as noted above, to a personal acquaintance or, at least, to "the friend of a friend." Similarly, party identification must be viewed differently when set in a non-partisan system, the specific goal of which is to blur partisan lines. Issue orientation is most directly relevant, but here, too, the character of the issues may suggest important qualifications. Verification of the general feeling that personality factors predominate in influencing city elections must await the use at the local level of survey research techniques employed in *The Voter Decides*.

had been a campaign issue in 10 cities. Respondents from 26 cities listed expansion, annexation, growth, and city-county relations; vice, gambling, law enforcement, and the police department; liquor control and local option; traffic, parking, and freeway location; zoning or industrial expansion; bond issues, public building, and facilities; and public works and drainage.

As for the six cities, too, personality factors were stressed. In Fresno, the platforms of all candidates were similar. A voter basing his choice on written statements, would have had a difficult time. In Chico, the only active candidate ran on a feminist platform, declaring that after thirty years it was time for a woman to be elected and promising only to do her best. Even in Berkeley, with its hotly contested and partisan-structured contests, a glance at the pamphlets sent to voters indicated the emphasis on qualifications, memberships, and background, rather than on programs and platforms. The "issues" when stressed at all were generally broadly defined: "I pledge to handle council business with common sense and integrity, to offer a fresh approach to unsolved problems." Candidates and campaigns in other cities could be described similarly. Pomona and Maywood provided examples of the influence a single person—in or out of office—might have on the local political structure over a long period. In each case, the personal dominance transcended programs or issues, was not based on traditional machine, boss, or party rule, and seemed related to the informal state of local politics.

An important qualification, however, must be made of this description of "issueless" politics. Every one of the six cities provided recent examples of campaigns that turned as much on policies and programs as on personalities. The 1949 election of Mayor Dunn in Fresno, related to the vice issue, is a dramatic example that received national publicity. Dunn's qualifications and personality were not nearly as important as his stand for closing up the town. In Berkeley, similarly, the mayoralty upset of 1947 was at least partly the result of resentment against the incumbent's machinations over the city managership. Even in tiny Maywood, in the heart of metropolitan Los Angeles where the important questions of community life are not subject to city control, recent elections have at least partly turned on such questions as the candidates' attitude toward parking meters and park expansion. In Pomona, a recent candidate rode to victory on the coat tails of a campaign against a council-manager charter, and in Chico and San Leandro new-broom tickets were victorious in campaigns stressing the general need for more vigorous community action to meet problems of growth.

In sum, there is clear evidence that local election politics generally emphasize personalities over issues but, when community consensus is absent and when programs and policies of local government become objects of concern, candidates may rise or fall not because of their qualifications or personalities, but because of their stand on the burning issue of the day.

RECAPITULATION

Local election campaigns are featured by their informality and the absence of permanent and continuing campaign organizations. Especially in small cities, successful electioneering goes to those persons and groups who can best derive benefits from "the politics of acquaintance," the almost unidentifiable by-product of the informal communication of organized community life. In all cities, however, formal political devices are also employed, and in all but the smallest cities "the politics of group mobilization" are important. The range of activity and the use of paid publicity and related expenditures depend not only on the size of the community but on such factors as tradition, geographical location, and personalities.

Campaigns are centered on individuals. Candidate slates are frequent, but individual campaigns separately identified, organized, administered, and financed are the rule. Groups, leaders, and coalitions change—frequently overnight; this fluidity appears more pronounced than in the more structured partisan state or national elections. Personalities are usually more important than issues in local elections. However, there are frequent examples in which the election turns upon questions of public policy or program.

9

Voters and Nonvoters

RESEARCH IN VOTING BEHAVIOR HAS GENERALLY IGNORED the city election. One probable reason for this, in California at least, is the absence of adequate registration and election statistics. No state record indicates the registration and partisan distribution in California cities, and local registration records are not always complete. In some small cities, for example, it may be necessary to add the figures for each precinct to determine the partisan registration for the city as a whole. The results of the local elections are more easily obtained, but not always in adequate detail.

Despite these shortcomings, election data were obtained which proved suggestive for future research if not always conclusive in their own right. It is not known how typical the small sample of six cities is of the state's cities. It was not considered possible to solicit corroborating evidence by the questionnaire, nor does published material exist to which to refer. Generalization, then, must be limited to the six cities.

WHO VOTES?

Three questions were asked about voter participation:

What is the difference in numbers and composition between the registered voters in city and state or national elections?

What is the difference in participation between city and state or national elections?

What is the difference in the internal composition of the electorate between city and state or national elections?

The Local Registration Roll.—In every even-numbered year, following the November state or national elections, county registrars throughout California clear from the rolls those who failed to vote in the preceding general and primary elections. Continually, attempts are made to screen out those who have moved or died. For cities holding elections in the spring of the

TABLE 47

DECLINE OF REGISTRATION ROLE
AFTER 1954 GENERAL ELECTIONS
(Spring, 1955)

City	Per cent decline
Chico	23
Fresno	19
Pomona	28
Maywood	32
San Leandro	23
Berkeley	25

odd-numbered years following this screening of the rolls, the net effect is a reduction in the number of eligible voters of 20 to 30 per cent. The figures in table 47 indicate the extent to which the electorate eligible to vote in a municipal race in the spring is reduced below the figure of the preceding November election.[1]

Only in Pomona did the decline in the number of registrants affect the two parties differently, and even in that city the margin was slight, the Democratic registration declining by 31 per cent, the Republicans by 26 per cent. The other five cities showed no difference between the two parties greater than one per cent. Generally speaking, the internal partisan distribution of the registration roll in a municipal race resembles that of the general election. Whether there are other than partisan differences between the groups eligible to vote in local and state or national elections remains a topic for future research.

TABLE 48

PARTISAN DISTRIBUTION OF PRECINCTS, 1955

Per cent precinct registered Democratic[a]	Per cent of total number of precincts					
	Berkeley	Chico	Fresno	Maywood	Pomona	San Leandro
0-34	16	3	0	0	9	5
35-44	20	26	2	0	26	13
45-54	22	32	11	0	31	17
55-64	15	32	27	17	27	29
65-100	27	7	60	83	7	36
TOTAL	100	100	100	100	100	100
City-wide Democratic average[a]	52	50	67	69	50	61

[a] Democratic per cent of two-party registration.

Internal patterns of party strength.—In the six cities, the Democratic percentage of the two-party registration varied from 50 in Chico and Pomona to 69 in Maywood. Within each city, too, the distribution of party strength throughout the community varied widely, as shown in table 48.

_____

[1] The data above have, of course, only indirect significance for Maywood and San Leandro, which hold their local elections in the spring of even-numbered years preceding the state and national elections. It remains to be ascertained whether and in what way the spring roll of an even-numbered year differs from that in the odd-numbered year—whether, for example, the normal registration drives preced-

Precincts differ in size, of course, both within each city and between cities. The table is accurate only in the broadest sense, yet it does serve to illustrate the widely varying patterns of distribution of party strength. Of the six cities, Chico represents the nearest approximation to a city evenly divided between the two parties with party strength widely dispersed throughout the community: 90 per cent of the precincts fall into the 35–64 per cent Democratic range. In contrast, Berkeley, also divided rather evenly between the two parties for the city as a whole, has only 57 per cent of its precincts in this middle range.

Such contrasting patterns suggest, of course, not only political, but social and economic differences. The pattern of organization and leadership of the two parties would also be expected to vary under the two sharply contrasting situations. One hypothesis might be that the existence of two large areas in a city, one heavily registered Republican, the other equally Democratic, would result in more partisan activities than if party strengths were diffused throughout the community. This might well affect city elections as well as partisan races.

Whether the data provide in part an explanation for the partisan situation in Berkeley remains a subject for further investigation. It is clear, however, that city-wide averages can often be as

TABLE 49

DECLINE OF VOTER TURNOUT FROM 1954 GENERAL ELECTION
TO 1955 CITY ELECTION

(Based on 1954 General Election Registration)

| City | Per cent turnout | | Per cent decline |
	General election	City election	
Chico	69	45	35
Fresno	70	48	34
Pomona	67	40	41
Maywood	62	43 (1954)	30
San Leandro	73	29 (1954)	60
Berkeley	67	43	36

ing state and national elections have enough impact in the early spring to increase the potential electorate for the municipal election. If this is true, it would be expected that the smaller general-law cities in California, which hold their elections in even-numbered years, would have a higher proportion of the citizenry eligible to vote than the generally larger charter cities, most of which hold their elections in the odd-numbered years.

misleading as they are informative and can mask wide internal variations in political behavior.

The Turnout for Local Elections.—If the number of those eligible to vote is somewhat smaller for the city race, the number of those who actually vote is substantially less, as table 49 indicates.[2] With the exception of the San Leandro vote, the consistency in table 49 is striking. (Besides, the figures for San Leandro are not typical. For example, in the three previous San Leandro city elections, the percentage turnout had been 42, 45 and 43 per cent.) In the typical local election, then, 40 to 50 per cent of the electorate (based on the general-election registration) will vote, as contrasted with a vote of 60–80 per cent in a state election. In other words, from 30 to 50 per cent of those who vote in the general election typically fail to participate in the municipal contest.[3] The data indicate that in a given city participation in

---

[2] Comparisons between municipal and state or national election turnout frequently ignore the difference in the base figure of those eligible to vote. Turnout percentages based on the smaller city-election registration are thus inflated when compared to participation in state or national races. In this analysis, a common base figure is used.

[3] Roscoe Martin had commented on the implications of this relatively low level of participation in his case study of Austin, Texas. He noted that the five winning candidates to the city council polled an average vote of 56.6 per cent of the total vote cast, 29.5 per cent of the electorate, 10.9 per cent of the potential electorate, and 6.9 per cent of the population. "This may be democracy, or as close an approximation as the typical community is able presently to achieve, but it patently is not the traditional American democracy whose dogmas so long have been familiar to the man on the street." "The Municipal Electorate: A Case Study," *Southwestern Political and Social Science Quarterly,* XIV (December, 1933), 193.

An interesting problem arises in attempting to explain the lower participation in municipal elections in view of these findings reported by DeGrazia. To the question, "Do you care a good deal who wins?" western respondents replied as follows with reference to the various elections:

RESPONDENTS CARING "VERY MUCH" OR "PRETTY MUCH"
WHO WINS THE ELECTION

Type of election	Per cent of respondents
Presidential	66
State	54
Local	58

De Grazia comments: "Almost a third of all voters possess little or no interest in who wins. Moreover, only about ten per cent fewer people claim an interest in state and local elections than in national elections, contrary to the general belief that interest in state and local elections is much less than in national elections. How this finding can be reconciled with the great difference between participation in presidential and state level elections is hard to say. Perhaps the public

local elections is higher where a separate mayoralty contest takes place and also in cases of a runoff.

These general findings are consistent with the results of O'Rourke's survey of voting participation in the cities of Los Angeles County.[4] There, over a seventeen-year period, the turn-out of voters at state and national elections had ranged from 68.4 to 86.6 per cent with an average for all 45 cities of 77.2 per cent. The turnout in municipal elections over the same period ranged from 10.3 to 60.9 per cent (based on the spring-registration roll), the average for all cities being 41.1 per cent. (The average for city elections would, of course, be lower and more comparable if based on the general-election registration.) The study indicates that there is no relationship between high voting performance in city elections and in state or national elections. O'Rourke states: "We may not conclude that because there is a good turnout of voters for municipal elections, there will be a good turnout at elections for state and national offices. The reverse is likewise true."[5]

Fluctuations in participation.—O'Rourke, speaking of Los Angeles County cities generally, asks whether the fluctuation in turn-out in local elections over a period of time is greater than that in presidential or state elections. He states that, "percentages of the registered electorate [voting] remain fairly constant in each city for almost all municipal elections. This may be contrasted with the somewhat more erratic percentages found in voting for state and national offices. . . . The evidence leads one to believe that there is a small core of citizens in each city who sustain municipal government."[6]

---

is more open to persuasion in a national campaign and more vulnerable to the great publicity attendant upon it. This puzzle must be left without any satisfactory theory to explain it." De Grazia, *The Western Public: 1952 and Beyond* (1954), p. 172. And so, it may be added, must be the puzzle as between state and local elections.

While relatively low local political interest and participation are undoubtedly prevalent throughout the United States, the pattern may be reversed under different cultural conditions. In a small French village, municipal contests consistently drew more voters by as much as one-third than did national elections. "The people of Peyrane are more interested in local situations and in each other as individuals than in political parties and national issues." Wylie, *Village in the Vaucluse* (1958), p. 233.

---

[4] O'Rourke, *Voting Behavior in the Forty-Five Cities of Los Angeles County* (1953).

[5] *Ibid.*, p. 5.

[6] *Ibid.*, p. 6.

The general finding does not hold for Pomona and Maywood, also in Los Angeles county. In both cities, variations in turnout in local races during a 25-year period (excluding the war years) exceeded the variation in state and national elections. In Berkeley, the only other city of the study for which adequate data have been gathered by local officials, turnout in presidential races between 1932 and 1957 varied from 77 to 84 per cent, a difference of 7 per cent; for municipal races, participation varied from 21 to 58 per cent, a range of 37 per cent. Until further evidence is developed, definitive conclusions on this matter must be held in abeyance. It seems likely that the variety of local conditions during a period of time, the absence of competition, or the irregular intensity of some civic issue, for example, would lead to a greater fluctuation in municipal turnout than in either state or national elections. Participation in the latter would probably be more consistent, because of partisan considerations.

Intracity differences in turnout.—As noted above, precinct data are frequently of little value in explaining neighborhood behavior; boundaries are artificial, the registration rolls are dated and the precincts vary considerably in size, all making comparison difficult. Nevertheless, an examination of the range of participation among the several precincts in a city may provide some insight into the variety of political behavior in a community. Table 50 suggests this.[7]

TABLE 50

Lowest and Highest Precincts: Per Cent Turnout of Registered Voters
(1954 General Election and 1954 or 1955 City Election Turnout
Based on 1954 General-Election Registration.)

City	General election			City election		
	Low	High	Range	Low	High	Range
Chico	56	89	33	49	71	22
Fresno	40	94	54	33	83	50
Pomona	48	81	33	24	72	48
Maywood	54	73	19	23	54	31
San Leandro	57	91	34	18	43	25
Berkeley	39	86	47	15	71	56

[7] In the table, the registration roll on which the city-election turnout was based was the April city roll except in Maywood, where the primary roll of the following June was used, and in Berkeley, where the general election roll of the preceding November was used.

The dangers in using city-wide averages are clear. The typical turnout for each of the six cities fell within the 40–50 per cent range, giving an impression of similarity. However, the internal distribution of voter participation indicates a different pattern among the several cities. In Chico, with a city-wide turnout of 69 per cent, precincts ranged from 56 to 89 per cent. In Fresno, precincts ranged from 40 to 94 per cent, while the city figure was 70 per cent. Clearly, wide discrepancies in participation between neighborhoods may provide more cause for concern than a generally low turnout throughout the city. The latter may merely indicate satisfaction with the status quo, but the former neighborhood frustration and alienation from the city government.

Partisan Differences in the Electorate.—It has been long asserted that Republicans vote in greater proportion to their potential strength than Democrats. This is primarily related to the differing social and economic characteristics of the two groups, but Lane notes that even when these factors are held constant, "Democrats are less likely than Republicans to be interested or concerned about the outcome of an election [or] . . . to follow up their interest with appropriate participation." [8] No direct testing of this widely held belief was attempted, but an analysis was made to investigate whether predominantly Republican precincts had a higher rate of voter participation than Democratic precincts in terms of the per cent of registrants voting.[9]

Excluding Maywood, because its small size permits no meaningful analysis, the data suggest this to be true for both state and city elections in four of the remaining five communities. Precincts which are relatively more Republican exercise a greater influence in elections, because of their relatively higher participation, than predominantly Democratic precincts. When the decline in vote from the state election to the municipal election is related to partisan registration, precincts registered more heavily Republican tend to decline the least. In short, the relationship between

---

[8] Lane, *Political Life* (1959), p. 144.

[9] Participation measured in terms of the percentage of registrants voting is not entirely satisfactory. For example, it is strongly held that Republican-tending persons register in greater numbers proportionately than Democratic-tending persons; registration, not voting, may be the crucial act of political participation. If this is true, participation data based on a registration base would tend to overstate the Democratic turnout in terms of the party's *potential* strength and to understate the Republican,

Republican registration and participation is greater in municipal elections than in state elections.[10]

The generalization cannot be extended without qualification to any particular city. In Berkeley, for example, precincts registered preponderantly with either party participated most heavily in the elections under investigation, while the more evenly divided precincts had a relatively weaker record. Heavily Republican precincts continued to participate in proportionately larger numbers than Democratic precincts, however, consistent with the general finding. In Fresno, for reasons unknown, the pattern of participation shows no relationship to precinct registration.[11]

VOTING BEHAVIOR

Do successful candidates for local office draw their support, relatively, from the same precincts? What relationships exist in the location of voting strength among candidates for partisan office

---

[10] A recent study of the Detroit area supports this finding. Two-thirds of Republicans surveyed in that study participated in local elections as compared with less than half of the Democrats. And whereas about 60 per cent of the Republicans had voted in all three elections (national, state, and local) during a three-year period, only about 40 per cent of the Democrats had done so. Although not directly stated, there appears no doubt that much of the drop-off occurred in the local elections. Eldersveld, *Political Affiliation in Metropolitan Detroit* (1957), pp. 39-41.

However, conflicting evidence is found in an as yet unpublished study of the Boston region conducted by Harvard graduate student Samuel Speck: "My study of nonpartisanship in Boston suggests that the finding that Democratic registrants turn out proportionately less for nonpartisan city elections than for state and national elections as compared to Republican registrants is not necessarily true in all political environments. Republicans seem to feel that participation in city elections is futile and accordingly their participation falls from the state and national turnout more than does that of Democratic wards." (Letter to the writer, dated February 15, 1960.)

[11] A recently reported study of four Michigan nonpartisan cities comes to a parallel conclusion that generalization concerning the causes and character of participation must be qualified. "Our hypothesis that Democrats would be least inclined to participate in local nonpartisan elections, while having some general validity in the four cities, must stand as a qualified generalization at best. Voter turnout seems to be related to ethnicity, whether councilmen are elected by wards or at large, to the degree to which voters regard themselves as having a meaningful stake in the election, and probably to other factors. The narrowness of our sample suggests that we should report our findings only as case studies. Nonvoting at the local level seems to be a matter requiring multivariate analysis." Williams and Adrian, "The Insulation of Local Politics Under the Nonpartisan Ballot," *American Political Science Review*, LIII (December, 1959), 1061.

and city candidates designated by local observers as well-known party members?

In Chico, party and local vote appeared to be related. Republican Mayor Meriam ran most strongly in areas in which Republican Governor Knight had done well, while the vote for Democratic Councilwoman Conley had a relationship with that for Democratic gubernatorial candidate Graves. However, the fact that Meriam obtained in no precinct less than 75 per cent nor Conley less than 53 per cent of the total vote cast suggests that party was not an important consideration in this election. In Fresno, the areas which strongly supported Mayor Dunn, an active Republican, were clearly the ones that had voted for Knight. But the uncertainty of reading partisan overtones into this fact was suggested by the discovery that Democratic trade unionist Wills—and in fact *all* winning commission candidates, regardless of party affiliation—had similarly received their strongest vote in this same Republican area of the city, although none of the candidates had participated in a slate campaign.

In Pomona, where the Republican party organization and leadership was described as active in city-election campaigning, a strong relationship existed between the vote for Knight and the vote for Republican mayor Cox, the candidate supported by the local G.O.P. Similarly, the location of the vote of Cox and winning council candidate Baker showed a strong relationship although they were bound only by informal ties. No active Democrat existed for purposes of comparison, but other relationships significant to the Pomona context were found. Cox and Turney, who were vocal and active opponents on the charter issue which featured the 1955 campaign, drew their support from those parts of the city which supported or opposed the proposed charter amendments. The anticharter areas were strongly Democratic, but the absence of direct partisan overtones was suggested by the fact that Turney, who ran most strongly in these precincts, was a Republican whose victory appeared to be a result of riding the coat tails of the anticharter movement.

In San Leandro, the apparent absence of partisan motivations was confirmed by the analysis of voting data. The area of support for Republican mayor Knick showed no relationship with that of Knight. Improvement-association politics determined the location of voting strength, not party considerations. This was also revealed by the close relationship in the source of voting support for two councilmen—one a Democrat, the other a Republican—who successfully conducted a joint-slate campaign.

In neighboring Berkeley, where the campaign had been described as partisan in every aspect but the form of the ballot, voting behavior also appeared strongly partisan. Cross, Cohelan, and Wilson, who were informally regarded as constituting a Democratic slate, all ran in direct relationship to the partisan voting behavior expressed in the state election five months earlier. In South Berkeley, an area strongly Negro and Democratic in composition, voters heavily supported both Negro candidates, although one was an active Republican, but tended to support only Democratic white candidates. In all other areas of the city, the vote for the two Negroes followed partisan lines.

The most important fact arising from the Berkeley analysis, however, concerned the shift in support over an eight-year period for the mayor. Coming to office in 1947 as a basically nonpartisan candidate running in a quasi-reform campaign, he had won support in all areas of the community. Of the 26 census tracts in the city, for example, he had carried all but two by a majority vote. Leaving office in 1955 as a highly partisan Democratic personality, he carried only seven of the 24 tracts in which he had previously won a majority; in certain tracts, the decline in support from 1947 to 1955 exceeded 30 per cent. Whereas in 1947 his vote had had no partisan significance, in fact negatively corresponded with the 1940 Roosevelt vote, his support in 1955 was strongly Democratic. This record suggests a hypothesis for future study, namely, that the vote for a candidate for nonpartisan office, running without the benefit of party label, may be subject in succeeding elections to much greater fluctuation than would be true in partisan contests. In the latter instance, the party label on the ballot may serve as a restraint on large-scale fluctuations in the vote for a particular candidate from one election to the next.

Group Voting Behavior in City Elections.—The state-wide survey solicited opinions on this question: "Do you have reason to believe that the members of any groups or people living in particular areas in your city tend to vote together for the same candidates in *city* elections?" The question was followed by a listing of such groups (residents of the more fashionable sections, members of the same religion, etc.).

Of the 192 cities replying to the questionnaire request, 132 (69 per cent) indicated that one or more groups in their city tended to vote together, 23 indicated "don't know," and 37 failed to answer this question or did not check any group. Generally speaking, as table 51 shows, the larger the city the more likely it was that one or more groups were reported as voting together.

TABLE 51

FREQUENCY OF REPORTED GROUP VOTING BEHAVIOR

Size of city	Total number of cities	Per cent of cities reporting groups vote together
Less than 5,000	53	53
5,000–50,000	119	73
50,000 and more	20	85
TOTAL	192	69

Some groups were noted more frequently than others, as suggested by table 52.

TABLE 52

TYPES OF GROUPS VOTING TOGETHER

(Replies from 192 Cities)

Group	Per cent of cities reporting groups vote together
Old-timers	46
Members of the same religion	28
Well-to-do residential sections	26
Business community	21
Lower-income residential sections	17
National or foreign-language groups	15
New subdivisions or tracts	13
Racial minorities	13
Democrats	4
Republicans	3
Other	4

NOTE: In several instances this analysis fails to discriminate between cities where the various groups exist, whether or not they vote together, and cities where no representatives of the particular group exist. For example, it may be that only 15 per cent of the 192 cities replying *have* identifiable national or foreign-language groups and that these groups vote together 100 per cent of the time.

Table 53 indicates the distribution of the groups according to the size of city, showing again the tendency of larger cities to report group voting more often. Two aspects of tables 52 and 53

TABLE 53

Percentage of 192 Cities Reporting Groups Voting Together

(By Size of Cities and Type of Group)

Percentage of cities reporting	Size of city (Number of cities)			
	Under 10,000 (90)	10,000-25,000 (57)	25,000-50,000 (25)	50,000 and over (20)
50 and above	Old-timers		Old-timers	
40-49		Old-timers	Same religion	Well-to-do Old-timers
30-39			Businessmen	Businessmen Lower income Same religion Racial minority
20-29	Same religion	Well-to-do Same religion Lower income	New subdivision Well-to-do	New subdivision National group
10-19	Businessmen Lower income National group	Businessmen National group Racial minority	Lower income National group Racial minority	
0-9	New subdivision	New subdivision		

appear particularly noteworthy: First, the frequency with which the group classed as "old-timers" is mentioned, second, the relative frequency of "members of the same religion." These suggest traditional and social groupings not always revealed by a statistical mapping of the geographical location of the vote and point up possible distinctions to be kept in mind when comparing local and state or national voting behavior.[12]

---

[12] In one California city (with a population of 30,000) the major differentiating factor reported in local politics was the occasionally contrasting interests and views of the home-owner versus the occupant of rental property, the two groups living in different parts of the city. In another community (population 22,000), the respondent noted: "We have a growing politically conscious group of retired citizens [not old-timers in the sense of long residence, necessarily]. . . . In my opinion this is to be a growing national and state problem and the elder is not lightly to be dismissed at election time. Many of this group have lost interest in

RECAPITULATION

Because municipal elections are held in the spring, under California practice the registration roll of voters eligible to participate in city elections is generally 20 to 30 per cent smaller than that for a state or national election. The partisan composition of the rolls is not significantly altered by this fact, however. The distribution of party strength in the community varies widely from city to city, and these differing patterns may be significant in determining the political structure of the city.

From 30 to 50 per cent of the voters in state or national elections fail to vote in municipal contests. Here again, patterns of participation within the community vary considerably from city to city. Large variations in voter turnout between precincts may be more significant than levels of participation in the city as a whole.

Republicans exercise probably a greater influence in local elections, because of superior turnout at the polls, than they do in state elections, but party affiliation may be a secondary factor in this regard. This is suggested by the testimony of respondents throughout the state and observations in the six cities that political party affiliation is incidental to other more basic divisions as a source of political influence. Race, religion, social relationships, length and place of residence, and business contacts are the indi-

---

future planning and building—and despite grandchildren or children they vote down improvements, school bonds, etc."

A respondent from a small city (population 10,000) stated: "Our city is about as nonpartisan as could be in city elections, and so are our local papers and incumbents. Naturally, there is private discussion and selection on such bases as Republican–Democrat, Catholic–Protestant, rich "hill" folk–modest "flatlands" folk, business–commuter, etc." (The tendency not to view these differences as partisan is significant.)

These comments are consistent with the observations of Robert Wood concerning political life in the suburbs: "A pattern of conflict [often] exists between old residents and new, frequently intensified by ethnic, religious, and occupational differences. This conflict arises both in the election of local officials and in the politics of individual decisions, and though it may be subdued by the common aspirations of the rising middle-class and the desire 'to belong,' it is nonetheless quite real." *Suburbia: Its People and Their Politics* (1958), p. 178.

cators cited most often. In certain circumstances, however, partisan motivations themselves seem of decided importance despite the nonpartisan form of ballot.

10

Size, Growth, Location, and Structure

THE SIZE OF THE CITY

More than any other single factor, the population size of the community determines the character of local politics. As one moves from a small town to a large city, the "politics of group mobilization" becomes more important than the "politics of acquaintance," although the two are not always readily distinguishable. Formal political organization made necessary by the need to focus the campaign on the unaffiliated man in the street or housewife is more frequently found in larger communities. Accordingly, campaign costs in larger cities are greater, because emphasis is placed less on face-to-face politicking and more on the use of various campaign media.

These observations are borne out by the responses to the state-wide survey. With respect to almost every question raised, the population classification of the city strongly influenced the character of the answer. This emphasizes that "cities" cannot always be looked upon as a politically meaningful class. Nor can a common remedy be prescribed to cure the civic ills of all communities. Cities, like humans, require individual diagnosis and treatment. Particularly in a state in which, by law, a municipality can be a community of less than 1,000 or more than 2,000,000 the use of such terms as "average" or "typical" can be decidedly misleading.

Some important relationships between size and political environment revealed by the state-wide survey were:

> In very small cities (5,000 and less) fewer community groups were listed as politically relevant. (In many areas, this was an indication, no doubt, of the lack of existence of such groups rather than of their political inactivity.)
>
> The frequency of *organized* political activity appeared strongly dependent on the size of the city. Such activity was reported in only 11 per cent of the cities under 5,000, as contrasted with 28 per cent of the cities between 5,000 and 25,000, and 50 per cent of those above 25,000.
>
> *Informal* political activity was reported in 21 per cent of the cities under 5,000, 42 per cent of the cities from 5,000 to 50,000, and 75 per cent of the cities above 50,000.
>
> Press activity in local elections varied in frequency and importance depending on the size of the city. Many small cities have no separate newspaper, of course, or are served only by a weekly. In 32 per cent of the cities under 25,000 and 64 per cent of the cities above that size, the press was reported as active in "many" elections or "every" city election. And press support was considered more important in the larger cities: in 70 per cent of the cities below 50,000 in which the press was active, supported candidates were reported as winning "many times" or "always," in contrast to 95 per cent of the cities above that size.
>
> Naturally, and relating to the necessity for formal activity, the cost of election campaigns varied in proportion to the size of the city. The range of reported costs for cities of the

same size was very broad, however, indicating that size was but one of several conditioning factors.

Respondents from larger cities were more likely to report the existence of community group voting: In 53 per cent of the cities under 5,000, 74 per cent of the cities from 5,000 to 50,000, and 85 per cent of the cities over 50,000, one or more religious, racial, ethnic or other groups were described as voting together. (This indicated, of course, the *existence* of more groups in the larger cities as much as their tendency to vote together.)

Respondents from the larger cities more often reported that political party *organizations* were active in city elections: such activity was reported in only 2 per cent of the cities under 10,000, 13 per cent of those between 10,000 and 50,000, and 25 per cent of those above 50,000. Similarly, the larger the city the more frequently was it reported that political party *leaders* were active in city elections, the percentage ranging from 25 of the cities under 5,000 to 71 of the cities above 100,000. And the larger the city, the more frequently was it reported that local officials had run for state or national office: 11 per cent of the cities under 10,000, 42 per cent of the cities between 10,000 and 100,000, and 71 per cent of the cities above 100,000.

The larger cities of the state were more likely to have a higher proportion of Republican councilmen and mayors than the small cities: in the cities over 50,000, 80 per cent of the mayors and 68 per cent of the councilmen were Republicans in 1955. The corresponding figures for cities under 50,000 were 59 per cent and 57 per cent. These figures had changed only slightly by 1959.

In addition to these gross differences related to size, significant differences in detail were suggested in the survey. For example, depending on the size of the city, different groups were likely to be reported "helpful" in local election politics. The local newspaper, merchants, women's organizations, and, to a lesser degree, veterans' organizations were frequently reported in cities of all sizes. Service clubs, on the other hand, were so reported in only one city over 100,000. Lay church groups were most frequently reported in cities under 10,000, while improvement associations were reported most often in cities above this size, city employees in cities of more than 25,000, and labor unions in cities of more than 50,000.

Similarly, the frequency with which particular community groups were reported as "voting together" varied according to the size of city, related, of course, to the existence of the group as well as its political cohesiveness. For example, a far greater proportion of respondents from cities of 25,000 and more suggested that members of the same religion voted together in their cities than was indicated by respondents from smaller communities. "Old-timers" were reported as voting together in many cities of all sizes. Racial minorities were so reported frequently only in cities of 50,000 and more.

THE IMPACT OF GROWTH

The observations relating physical size to the character of local politics would undoubtedly be true in one form or another in almost any section of the nation. More peculiar to California is the impact of growth on the cities of the state. Population and areal changes of 100 per cent in a city in a ten-year period are not exceptional, and both the magnitude of change and the rate at which it has taken and continues to take place profoundly shape the political process. Growth brings with it the problems and pressures with which local politics are concerned—the conflict of personalities, the creation of new interest groups, and the change in the character of existing ones.

Added to growth as an influence on the community scene is the extraordinary rate at which change is taking place. In almost every community of the state, large segments of the population —in some new cities the entire population—are newcomers, and the adjustment of old and new is the dominant note. One important feature in many cities is the tendency of the large subdivisions, inhabited by hundreds of families virtually overnight, to organize themselves politically. Neighborhood localism and demands for representation leading at times to a district or ward system of elections are important phases in the political pattern accompanying growth.

Generalization is difficult, however. In each city, the impact of change is felt in a somewhat different way. Certain groups and interests are affected in one community but not in another. In San Leandro, for example, growth produced a struggle between new self-conscious residential subdivisions and the older established sections of the city, including among their members the economic leaders of the community. In Pomona, on the other hand, the pattern of residential development placed the newly developed sections of the city on the same side of the local political fence as the economic leadership of the city, with the older and poorer areas of the city in opposition. In Fresno, much of the growth was taking place outside the city limits, which created issues between city and county to a greater degree than in other communities.

Berkeley provided an example, not of rapid growth in absolute terms, but of a dramatic shift in the racial composition of the population within the city, a change which influenced the political structure as much as numerical growth. In Chico, pressures of internal and external change were only beginning to be felt within the political structure of the community itself, while in Maywood, the problems of growth related more to the place of the city in the metropolitan complex than to its internal political processes.

Despite this diversity, growth has been the single most important conditioning factor in recent California local politics.

THE GEOGRAPHICAL LOCATION OF THE CITY

Geographical location remains to be briefly mentioned. The contrast between Fresno and Berkeley is suggestive of but one facet of this more general problem: one city is the center of a large and important area, the other but a small part of a larger metropolitan complex. In Fresno, one studies a whole community, in Berkeley only a part of one. Politically, Fresno has within itself the power to solve most of its community problems, while Berkeley must seek solutions in concert with its neighbors. The relevance of this to local politics would appear to be in the nature of conditioning the state of mind. The impression is gained that local politics "mean more" in Fresno, with a resulting intensity of interest and importance attached to the election process.

THE FORM OF GOVERNMENT

Some central questions of local government concern the mayor, particularly under the council-manager form. Should he be appointed by the council or separately elected? What powers should he be given? In three of the six cities mayors were elected separately and in three appointed by the city council, hence some limited comparisons were possible. None of the mayors, however, possessed other than ceremonial powers, except that in Fresno, before the recent charter, the mayor was also public-safety commissioner.

Public participation at the polls was consistently higher in the elections for mayor than in elections where only council offices appeared on the ballot. In terms of community leadership, however, it was not clear that the elected mayors were in a stronger position or necessarily assumed one than their appointed counterparts in the remaining three cities. The leadership propensities and abilities of the incumbents in the six cities depended more on individual personality and community tradition than on the manner of selection. Nevertheless, the potential power for leadership in the mayor's office resulted in an intensity of organizational activity and interest and a more concentrated and vigorous attempt at recruitment than was true for council elections.

Generally the city manager's office had become a source of political power, although here too the pattern was varied, depending on the community or person. To some degree, in the four council-manager cities, the administrative head of the city had assumed responsibility for what might be designated "professional civic leadership." Under that term are included the anticipation and determination of city needs, their presentation to the council and to the public, and their implementation when accepted. The administrative head is an expert not only in the field of management techniques but, and probably more importantly, in the field of politics. It is clear, however, that the politics referred to are not the politics of election, the central focus of this study, but rather politics as defined in the dictionary, "the theory or practice of managing or directing affairs of public policy."

The manager's policy role has decided implications for the

election process. The manager regards it as one of his prime tasks to resolve conflict, to seek community consensus, to bring all elements of the city to a meeting of the minds. It is his job to raise the alternative viewpoints and suggest their reconciliation; in a sense, his success may be measured by the degree to which such conflicts are resolved before they become election issues. This study produced slight evidence that election campaigns were more "issue-oriented" in council-manager than in mayor-council cities, but a vigorous and able manager would frequently remove civic issues from controversy through their prompt resolution. The danger that such resolution might occur before adequate public consideration has taken place is not discounted, but public consideration is frequently more meaningful because it has been encouraged by the manager.

The positive role of the administrator in policy creation and development is not peculiar to the municipality, of course, and exists at every governmental level from the city to the United Nations. But given the low intensity of much of community politics, the degree of consensus on city needs and programs, and the apparent difficulties of recruitment of elected officials and their part-time responsibilities, this political role may assume a relatively greater importance in the city. This important factor of the community political structure must be kept to the forefront in any analysis. An awareness of the distinction between election and appointment of the key policy-creating official is clearly important for the understanding of local politics.

RECAPITULATION

Cities may have a common legal status, but each community is subject to individual environmental influences that shape its political institutions. Generalizations may disguise more than they disclose.

Cities with larger populations are more frequently and more intensively organized politically than smaller communities. The size of the city determines usually the types of active groups, whether organized formally or informally, as well as the probability of bloc voting. In the larger communities political party organizations and leadership are more active in nonpartisan elections, and the role of the press is considered more influential.

Local politics are further conditioned by the impact of growth and change, so typical of many California cities. The pressures may be external—the result of expanding city boundaries and increases in population; or they may be internal—resulting from turnover within the city's traditional boundaries. In any event, these changes shape the political forces within the community and equally the problems which the community must attempt to solve.

Cities similar in size and other characteristics may have dissimilar politics when one is a central city of, for example, a large rural area, and the other but a part of a large metropolitan complex. Politics in the latter appear to be more diffused and less intense, but facts are lacking to confirm this impression.

Finally, the form of local government is relevant for local politics. Electing a mayor provides a focus of political activity and interest, although this is not always reflected in the pattern of leadership following the election. In almost every council-manager community, the city manager has become a source of civic leadership, and this unquestionably introduces an important element into city election politics even though the manager himself is rarely directly involved.

THE APPRAISAL

11

The Politics of Nonpartisanship

"A STABLE DEMOCRATIC SYSTEM," WRITES AN EMINENT political sociologist, "requires sources of cleavage so that there will be struggle over ruling positions, challenges to parties in power, and shifts of parties in office; but without consensus—a system allowing the peaceful 'play' of power—there can be no democracy." [1] Competition and conflict on the one hand, consensus and cohesion on the other, these are the poles between which democracy must operate. These are the standards by which nonpartisanship must be measured if we are to understand its relevance for urban political life.

---

[1] Lipset, "Political Sociology," *in* Merton, ed., *Sociology Today* (1959), p. 113.

V. O. Key mirrors these views in his attempt to develop a measure by which the requisites of "adequate popular leadership" may be judged. With his attention focused on the state and national scene and on the system of political parties and admitting that "any set of standards must consist of more or less abitrarily stated criteria," Key places his emphasis on the central theme of "competition."

> On the American scene a high priority would generally be given to the requirement that the parties compete for power. Although the struggle for position must avoid the threat of resort to the sword and must not be so intense as to disrupt the social system, competition itself rates a high value as a protector of liberty and as a means for assuring responsiveness of government. A belief in the corrective efficacy of competition permeates American political thought as well as other aspects of American life.[2]

Thus, the stress is on competition, but competition within limits. The writers of *Voting* suggest this in their admonition that the classical model of democratic man, continually and rationally choosing between alternatives, does not fit the facts or needs of modern society if, in truth, it ever did. They continue:

> Liberal democracy is more than a political system in which individual voters and political institutions operate. For political democracy to survive, other features are required: the intensity of conflict must be limited, the rate of change must be restrained, stability in the social and economic structure must be maintained, a pluralistic social organization must exist, and a basic consensus must bind together the contending parties.[3]

One would add only the related thought, with reference to the present study, that the conditions and qualities basic to democratic society need not necessarily be identical at every level of government at any moment. For example, there should be little argument over the proposition that the absence of competition for power at the national level, even for a short time, would be fraught with grave consequences. The same cannot necessarily be

---

[2] Key, *American State Politics* (1956), p. 11.
[3] Berelson *et al.*, *Voting* (1954), p. 313.

said of the local community. One admittedly unique California city has had only two contested elections since the city was incorporated in 1913. It is well-governed, with a tradition of community service, and its legislative and administrative branches are clearly responsive to the wishes of the citizenry. Admittedly, in another time and place, such a record might well prove intolerable. On the other hand, local political conflict may become bitter and intense but still entail no risk of tearing the fabric of democracy because within the larger society there is a general consensus concerning political values. All of which underscores an obvious fact: the context in which the political process takes place cannot be ignored.

Nor, of course, is an election an end in itself, particularly in a democratic society. Its ramifications include such subjects as the councilmen's behavior after the election, the quality of the legislative product, and the character of the administration. This study, however, is concerned with the immediate and direct implications of the electoral system, not with its total impact.

The problem of making a general appraisal can be approached by posing questions relevant to the criteria of competition and consensus and then endeavoring to answer them on the basis of the evidence accumulated by this study.[4]

The questions are these:

> 1. Does everyone have free and equal access to public office and opportunity for political activity? As a corollary, are there adequate opportunities for the meaningful expression of dissent, for the formulation of protests against the "powers that be" through the presentation of opposition candidates and programs?
>
> 2. Do social, economic, racial, or religious factors in local political life significantly impinge upon competition and

---

[4] Janowitz and Marvick have evaluated the 1952 presidential election "in terms of the requirements for maintaining a democratic society." See "Competitive Pressure and Democratic Consent," *in* Eulau *et al.*, *Political Behavior* (1956), pp. 275–286. In this analysis the authors offer five criteria to assess when an election produces a "process of consent" which contributes to effective representative government. Elements of the criteria are included in several questions posed in the text. However, the criteria are not all relevant to local elections, particularly in the smaller cities and towns. In addition, several criteria can be evaluated only on the basis of extensive public-opinion polling of a social-psychological nature, an alternative not available in this study. The authors demonstrate, however, how empirical research may be used to evaluate complex and elusive questions of the sort here posed.

the sense of community cohesion and affect the claim to representativeness on the part of elected officials?

3. Are votes for individual candidates made meaningful by the identification and clarification of candidates' views on the relevant current issues facing the city? Are programs for municipal action developed and presented so that there can be "programmatic competition" as well as candidate competition?

4. Are men and women of integrity and ability entering public office? Does the electoral process produce the kind of community leadership esssential to the progress and well-being of the city?

For each of these questions two sub-questions are posed: (1) What is the condition existing? (2) What is the relationship between the electoral system—in this case the nonpartisan form of ballot—and the condition? It is obvious that the second question is more difficult to answer than the first, particularly in the absence of comparative data on experience under other forms of elections.

Question 1: *Does everyone have free and equal access to public office and opportunity for political activity? As a corollary, are there adequate opportunities for the meaningful expression of dissent, for the formulation of protests against the "powers-that-be" through the presentation of opposition candidates and programs?*

Judged by the regularity of contests, the presence of large numbers of candidates, the ability of local groups to sponsor and elect candidates, the frequency with which incumbents are ousted, and the almost total absence of any evidence of obstructions deliberately placed in the way of political activity, the answer to both questions, *as qualified below*, appears to be strongly in the affirmative. With a frequency and variety perhaps unique to the local political scene, individual candidates enter the lists either on their own or with the support of some group, often with surprising success.

The word "adequate" in the second question implies the existence of some objective standard for measurement. None, of course, exists. It is apparent, however, from a review of the six-city experience that in every city, during a relatively limited period, the "outs" have been successful in opposing the "ins." In some cities, this has been evidenced by a change in mayors or in the composition of the council. At times, the opposition has taken some particular administration program to the people and been successful in defeating it. At times such movements have been negative, the "outs" wishing only to preserve the status quo, but on other occasions the "outs" demanded and got action against the wishes of the incumbents. The channels required to effectuate such protests vary. In Chico, little more than word-of-mouth discussion featured the postwar shift in power; at the other extreme, an extensive and costly campaign, rivaling a presidential contest in its local impact, accompanied the famous Fresno clean-up of 1949.

Certain aspects of the nonpartisan system of elections would appear to support, if not explain, these phenomena. The freedom from a requirement of organized support, which is implicit in the system, the ease of nominating procedures, the removal of the barrier to service or activity which a party designation on the ballot might create, and the generally modest cost of an election campaign in all but the largest cities—all these point to a positive relationship between the form of elections and the facts described. On the other hand, there is probably little question that under a traditional partisan system competition is more formalized, leading to the possibility, at least, that more frequent and consistent channels may be established for the airing of opposing viewpoints. That meaningful competition and opposition are more plentiful under a partisan system has not yet been established, however, and any such generalization must be seriously qualified by the existence of many cities in which one party has a preponderant majority and cannot be effectively challenged.

Question 2: *Do social, economic, racial or religious factors in local political life significantly impinge upon competition and the sense of community cohesion and affect the claim to representativeness on the part of elected officials?*

Models of an ideal democratic society are based on the notion that in the race for public office all contenders should start from the same mark and run on the same track. Acceptance of this ideal is a precondition for the development of individual and group consensus to which Lipset and Berelson refer. It is obvious, however, that at all levels of government many participants are handicapped in such a contest and must run a considerable distance before even reaching the starting line. A few favored participants may even have a head start. Pertinent to this inquiry is not the question of fair chances everywhere, however, but simply whether *special* hurdles or advantages exist in the local political process, particularly elections. What light is shed on the matter from this examination of local elections?

From the standpoint of election to office and active participation in civic affairs, barriers of the types suggested clearly exist. Residence on the wrong side of the tracks, a low-income job providing little time or opportunity for civic activity, lack of education, skin color of a darker hue than that of the majority, or religious belief of which many disapprove and more do not understand—these factors constitute hurdles. The reverse side of the coin is that the white, Protestant, male, reasonably well-off, who lives on the right side of the tracks, shares similar advantages in political participation that he likely enjoys in other sectors of society. However, these factors appear less decisive in the political sphere. In fact, the political process seems a key force in the long-range reduction of their importance, as the following discussion suggests.

Social barriers peculiar to local politics are difficult to identify. Differences in dress, speech, and habit are, of course, politically relevant but no more so than in other areas of community life. Economic barriers relate primarily to the part-time and generally low-paid nature of public office. The time and expense necessary to campaign and serve preclude many from political activity. This is an occupational as well as an economic problem. Certain jobs —regardless of wage or salary—permit the time off that public life requires; others do not. The rising young middle-class professional man, for example, would probably suffer greater financial loss than a blue-collar employee. Again, however, these types of hurdles are not peculiar to local politics but hamper participation in many other areas of community affairs.

The principal religious barrier to local public office apparent in the course of this investigation is that raised against Roman Catholics. Many Protestants report a reluctance to support Catholics for local office or, at least, a recognition that religion is something to be considered. The relevance of Catholic faith to educational matters rather than to municipal government has often been suggested, but the latter was not excepted from consideration. This religious factor is probably more important in small communities, one suspects, and in these the religious barrier may remain higher in the political sphere than in other areas of community life.

The reverse is likely to be true of racial or related ethnic barriers. Social acceptance of Negroes, for example, appears far behind political acceptance in the two cities, Fresno and Berkeley, where this group constitutes an important minority of the population. It could even be argued that in certain instances a person's minority status had provided an advantage in his political career. The very solidarity produced by the minority condition of the group gave its representatives or leaders a measure of support often lacking among their white counterparts.[5] For the group as a whole the barrier was still high, however, as indicated by the fact that in neither city has a Negro ever been elected to municipal office, although in Berkeley one missed only by the margin of a few hundred votes.

One hurdle not suggested so far is sex. In most cities, elective municipal office is considered a man's job and women rarely compete. Whether this results from the reluctance of women to stand the gaff of public service or from their husbands' reluctance to see their fireside unprotected is not clear.

Politically *favored*, on the other hand, are those segments of the community which are characterized by formal or informal organization and patterns of communication. Among these groups the business community along with, and often complemented by, the local press most frequently assume the greatest importance. Yet a great variety of other groups are active and influential: veterans' organizations, women's clubs, service clubs and lodges, improvement associations, labor unions, and lay church groups were among those most frequently mentioned.

With respect to voter participation, barriers and advantages are of a different, although related, character. In California, at least, there are no significant "built-in" obstacles to free and equal

---

[5] Lane supports these generalizations. Citing Kornhauser, he states that "although clearly subordinate, metropolitan Negroes feel fully as politically effective as do white citizens in a similar status and environment. . . . [This feeling of effectiveness arises] from the contrast between the political arena where the universal franchise grants to the Negro a degree of influence which he so clearly lacks in private life. And this attitude is supported by frequent public recognition of Negro power and ardent political solicitation of Negro votes." Lane, *Political Life* (1959), pp. 150–151.

participation in local elections. Registration is simple, precincts numerous, polling places convenient, and elections are honest. A minor qualification might be that transients or frequent movers are discriminated against by waiting periods before registration, but these are scarcely longer than required by administrative necessity. There are, therefore, no apparent obstacles to equal activity in this respect.

Nevertheless, voter participation in local elections is often distressingly low throughout the community and dangerously low in particular neighborhoods. Fewer than half of the registered voters actually participate in municipal elections; in the six cities participation in certain areas fell as low as 15 per cent. Universal adult participation in elections is not, of course, essential to democratic health. In fact, as Lipset indicates on the basis of German experience in the 1930's, "an increase in the level of participation may reflect the *decline* of social cohesion and the breakdown of the democratic process." [6] But, as Janowitz and Marvick point out, while nonvoters can act as a "cushion," if they are not overconcentrated in a particular social class, persistent nonvoting by a particular group in the community is perilous to the democratic process: "A consensus is incomplete and fragile which is produced without the active involvement of one social class or ethnic group." [7]

Nonvoting frequently correlates with the other types of political nonparticipation in terms of the groups and areas affected. This is not surprising, of course. Significant, though, is the conclusion, that nonvoting in these areas is proportionately greater in municipal elections than in state and national races. [8]

In what way does the existence of these differential barriers and advantages—social, racial, religious, economic—relate to the form of elections? Clearly, any relationship would be only incidental; the problems rest on more fundamental bases than the type of ballot employed. But does the absence of the party label

---

[6] "Political Sociology," *in* Merton, ed., *Sociology Today* (1959), p. 95.

[7] "Competitive Pressure and Democratic Consent," *in* Eulau *et al.*, *Political Behavior* (1956), p. 227. From an article previously printed by Institute of Public Administration, University of Michigan, 1956.

[8] The evidence of the Williams and Adrian study and the Boston report cited above, p. 140, as well as the record of participation in Berkeley municipal elections, make it clear that this generalization must be seriously qualified on the basis of present data.

and the supposed reduction of partisan activity increase the importance of these nonparty factors?

Here, unquestionably is the most critical and difficult question facing the student of nonpartisanship. To the nonpartisan advocate, Robert Lane throws these challenging assertions:

> The central theme of politics is group conflict. Where groups are organized under leaders of their own selection, political life will flourish—at least in the sense of broadened interest and participation. But it does not serve the interest of the dominant groups of a community to encourage the organization of the working class or ethnic groups, or wards and precincts other than those in which they live.
>
> . . . there are inherent contradictions in the middle—and upper-class ideals: universal political participation versus middle- and upper-class dominance.
>
> . . . the municipal reform ideal of non-partisan, efficient apolitical politics is certain to seem attractive to white, native Protestant, middle-class citizens. By abolishing party labels, the lower-status groups are disoriented and become the unwitting clients of the upper-status press.
>
> Municipal reforms of this nature: non-partisanship, smaller city councils, the replacement of mayors by city-managers, may serve admirable technical purposes and in the long run be in the best interests of most groups in the community— but they weaken the political ties of the disorganized and depressed groups in the community. And, in doing this, they serve a strong, but usually repressed, interest of the community "power-elite," whose focus is ostensibly upon the gains in efficiency and honesty brought about by the reforms, but who profit from the political apathy of the underdog.[9]

According to the Lane thesis nonpartisanship enhances the importance of nonparty groups; these groups tend to be dominated by those of higher socioeconomic status; lower-class citizens lack the political instruments to make their voices heard; consequently they lack representation in civic bodies; this leads to an attitude of alienation and frustration which reduces participation.

Neither Lane nor any other writer known to the author have produced evidence that would directly substantiate (or negate) assertions which posit such characteristics or effects to the non-

---

[9] Lane, *op. cit.*, pp. 269–271.

partisan system. Comparisons of participation, representation, feelings of alienation, and group influences on the political process under partisan and nonpartisan elections have not been made. The findings of the present study suggest that in the absence of formal political structure and activity, related to the nonpartisan ballot, the importance of nonparty groups is enhanced to some extent, but certainly the groups are more than proportionately active and influential in partisan contests as well. In some instances, too, these groups, for example trade unions, represent generally low-participation segments of the community and do become active in local politics.

In making comparisons to determine the impact of nonpartisan elections on the democratic process, it will be necessary to pursue the assertions made above to their logical conclusion; and to raise the question whether the political party is, can, or should be the vehicle by which the admittedly serious problem of differential participation and access to influence can be attacked. If the political party is a logical instrument, under what conditions can it best serve the interests of the local democratic process? And, assuming these conditions to exist, is a partisan primary or ballot at the local level essential or desirable?

To these questions, no ready answers or even clear lines of direction are available. However, one cannot assume that a stress on partisanship will automatically lead to an increase in participation and a strengthening of group ties to the community. Partisan advocates allege that many of the nonparticipants noted above identify themselves more with party groups than with the nonparty groups likely to be active in local politics. The conclusion drawn, therefore, is that if the parties were more overtly active, the nonparticipants would feel a greater identity with local politics and community affairs.[10] In the context of 1960, the Democratic party is more likely to be singled out in this regard than the Republicans.[11] It is also clear from studies of voting behavior in

---

[10] This conclusion is suggested by a study of a large-city election conducted by Alfred de Grazia. To the question, "Why was the election important to you?" 19 per cent of the Negro respondents replied "because of party," while only 10 per cent of the respondents in the city as a whole gave this reply. "The Limits of External Leadership Over a Minority Electorate," *Public Opinion Quarterly*, XX (Spring, 1956), 121.

[11] Cited above, p. 57, were data indicating that Democrats fared far better in partisan local elections (in New York and Indiana) than in nonpartisan races (in California).

presidential races that a heightening of partisanship may stimulate interest and participation. Yet Gunnar Myrdal notes "The tendency to cynicism which the author has observed everywhere in American Negro communities, becomes *strengthened* by the American party system, which does not correlate closely with broad divisions of real interests and social ideals." [12] A study of politics in Los Angeles emphasizes: "Political parties become institutionalized when they are accepted by people as performing an important and meaningful role in society. . . . In the case of the parties in Los Angeles, and in California as a whole, such a development has not taken place. . . . [The parties] are loosely moored to the social structures in which they exist. They seem to have largely failed as institutionalized agencies for channeling political demands." [13]

The same study points out that the Democratic party organization is strongest, in terms of leadership, active workers, clubs, and the like among the same types of persons who are already participants and leaders in the nonparty groups noted above, the middle- and upper-class citizens. The same would certainly be true of the Republican party.

To admit uncertainty about the solution for these shortcomings in the democratic process is not to sweep them under the rug. Problems of dangerously low participation, of substantial barriers to free and open participation in political life, of inadequate representation and of politically disoriented citizens exist. They stand as a challenge to advocates of nonpartisanship and partisanship alike. Their remedy demands more than altering the form of ballot. Whether the cure in any community would be aided by a strengthening of party organizations, or by an increase in activity of hitherto inactive or nonexistent nonparty groups, or by other possibilities is a matter for analysis, not for polemics and premature generalizations from the partisan or nonpartisan camp.

Question 3: *Are votes for individual candidates made meaningful by the identification and clarification of candidates' views on the relevant current issues facing the city? Are programs for municipal action developed and presented so that there can be*

---

[12] *An American Dilemma* (1944), p. 507 (my italics).
[13] Scigliano, "Democratic Political Organization in Los Angeles" (1952), pp. 17, 107.

"programmatic competition" as well as candidate competition?

During the study, impressions were gathered about the existence of issues and the presentation of programs to the electorate
by competing candidates. Nothing found in the course of the
inquiry would permit a judgment about the impact of these
factors on individual electoral choice. Local elections are probably
less frequently "issue-oriented" than state or national contests.
Relatively speaking, community consensus on many matters of
public policy is so strong, the constitutional and statutory restrictions under which such policies must be developed so extensive, and much of the business of local government so routine
that questions of program may often assume less importance than
the choice of personnel to implement them. In addition, the
presence of a city manager may insure the resolution of many
problems of community policy before they become campaign issues. Nevertheless, occasionally issues become important, candidates are labeled as to their position, and this position influences
the outcome of the election. The extent to which pressing community issues are not brought to the fore for public resolution is
undetermined. It is equally as difficult to evaluate whether a loss
in municipal effectiveness results from the reported absence of a
continuing and sustained presentation of alternative public policies over several elections.

Are nonpartisan elections less "issue-oriented" than partisan
contests? Do the latter provide more "programmatic competition,"
both of the moment and of a sustained variety, as well as competition merely between the candidates? Traditional theory suggests this should be so, with opposing party slates presenting contrasting municipal platforms which have continuity from year to
year. But Peter Odegard and E. Allen Helms remind us that,
"Political parties in the United States, whether they be viewed
nationally or locally, are not primarily interested in matters of
policy." [14] In support of this view, a study of a recent partisan
Chicago mayoralty campaign indicated that only 17 per cent of
the voters felt that the election was important "because of issues,"
while *all* respondents replied "because of a man I wanted." [15] On
the other hand, a study of four Michigan cities produced this

---

[14] *American Politics*, 2d ed., rev. (1947), p. 204.
[15] De Grazia, *op. cit.*, p. 121.

conclusion: "The more assiduously issues in the nonpartisan elections were pursued, the more the resulting vote conformed to the partisan pattern. The more issue-oriented the campaign, the higher the correlation between nonpartisan and partisan voting patterns." [16] In any event, existing evidence does not permit the prediction of a drastic change in the personality-issue orientation of the campaign with a return to the partisan ballot.

Instead, it seems likely that the basic mechanism for the presentation and resolution of public-policy questions will continue to be a resultant of a variety of forces, not always reflected in the election process. Community groups, both special-purpose and civic in character; the bureaucracy and administration of the government; the local newspaper; individual leaders in and out of public office; party politicians and organizations, even under a nonpartisan system; all will play a role. The issue turns not on whether the partisan ballot would basically redefine this pluralistic pattern of public-policy formulation and decision-making, for obviously the description fits any democratic society. Rather, the question is posed whether and in what manner the more overt and formal introduction of the political party into the arena would shape and alter existing processes and procedures. It is clear that under certain circumstances the political parties could contribute to a public awareness of local issues and present candidates responsible for a particular platform. But, on the evidence available, we have no clear basis for predicting that this would happen consistently and frequently.

Question 4: *Are men and women of integrity and ability entering public office? Does the electoral process produce the kind of community leadership essential to the progress and well-being of the city?*

These final questions by which one might evaluate the plan of nonpartisan elections against certain ideals of democratic practice have nothing to do, directly, with participation, representation, freedom of access, or group influence. Nevertheless, the practical matter of whether the political system attracts capable men and women into public office is as crucial to the maintenance of a free society as these other factors.

---

[16] Williams and Adrian, "The Insulation of Local Politics Under the Nonpartisan Ballot," *American Political Science Review*, LIII (December, 1959), 1058.

Integrity, ability, leadership are characteristics difficult to examine and to define. Yet, by and large, as one travels through the state, the quality of the elected officials of California cities appears impressive; their interest, dedication, and ability stand inspection. Some communities are more favored than others, of course, and many have crack-pot councilmen and mediocre mayors. Given the general disinterest of the electorate, however, one can only say that the public generally gets a better quality of local officials than it deserves.

Still, the problem remains. Few cities appear to have arrived at that happy state in which the recruitment of competent persons to serve their communities has ceased to be of importance. The apparent exclusion of women from equal consideration has substantially reduced the base of able and interested citizens who could hold office with distinction. And artificial restrictions of race, religion, and social or economic class may discourage or prevent persons of ability from seeking or holding office.

Contrasting arguments are raised about the relationship of the form of election to these problems. It is suggested on the one hand that the nonpartisan ballot encourages candidates to stand for office who would not otherwise engage in politics, and on the other that the absence of the more formalized political structure suggested by the partisan ballot removes a potent recruiting agency from the field. The experience gained in this study suggests that in California both arguments contain an element of truth. Desirable political party recruitment of able candidates for local office was discovered, even under existing nonpartisan conditions; at the same time many respondents indicated they would not have run for office if partisan considerations suggested by ballot labeling had been raised.

A SCORE CARD

How then does the nonpartisan election system in California measure up against these criteria of democratic practice? To the author, a score card appears this way:

"Pretty good" on general measures of competition, frequency of contests, opportunities for dissent and ability to "kick the rascals out."

"Pretty bad" on the participation of certain segments of the community, both in terms of membership in civic bodies and voting, with a resulting reduction in the representativeness of the local government.

"About average" on the presentation of candidates who offer issues and platforms to the voters for consideration.

"Above average" on the ability and integrity of elected public officials.

Would the score card be different in cities using the partisan election system? Evidence on which comparisons could be made would help provide the answer, but is not presently available.

12

The Principles of Nonpartisanship

DURING THE HALF-CENTURY WHICH HAS PASSED SINCE
the development of the nonpartisan ballot in the United States
the abolition of the party label in local elections has been extended to almost two-thirds of American cities—65,000,000 citizens. On the basis of this experience and the findings of this
study, what can now be said about the hopes and aims of the
advocates of nonpartisanship?

Let us review in turn the several arguments used by the "found-
ing fathers" of nonpartisanship and its supporters today, as set
forth in chapter ii, and examine their current relevance in the
light of actual practice. These various arguments represent neither

a formally developed nor an internally consistent philosophy. Some of the views, even those expressed by the same writer, are contradictory or inconsistent. By and large, the positions have been presented in the heat of political battle by partisan non-partisans rather than as the result of calm, empirical analysis. This is not to say that the arguments are false, nor to criticize those who have set them forth, but merely to clarify the circum-stances surrounding their origins and, in many cases, their con-tinued sponsorship.

1. *City government is largely a matter of "good business prac-tice" or "municipal housekeeping." The issues that come before the electorate and the city council are not really "political," and there is little room for "politics." Therefore, it is not necessary to establish organized political competition as suggested by the partisan ballot.*

The basis of this argument, which contains an element of truth, tends to prove too much. If carried to its logical extreme, these remarks would imply the lack of a need for elective officials at all. The basis of home rule and a local council responsive to the citizenry is that there *are* political questions to be decided. As Walker and Cave assert, "Politics, of course, remains the heart of local government—as it should." [1] It is logically inconsistent for advocates of home rule to talk about local government in non-political terms. If local affairs are truly nonpolitical, an assertion which this writer would deny, we should establish them as ad-ministrative responsibilities of some larger unit of government.

On the contrary, almost every one of the so-called "housekeep-ing" functions of municipal government is fraught with policy questions. While there may be "no Republican way to pave a street or Democratic way to operate a water works," there are important policy questions and alternatives involving even these seemingly mundane activities. Politics will inevitably shape their resolution. Where should streets be located, how much of the city's money should go into street improvements in any given year, what should be the responsibility of the subdivider in build-ing new streets, what portion of the water-supply costs should be met from tax funds, what should be the water rate differential between residential and industrial users, what policies should

---

[1] Walker and Cave, *How California is Governed* (1953), p. 226.

govern the extension of service into noncity areas—these are policy decisions for any community. They are worthy of the label "political" in the most complete sense of the term, and they pertain basically to "housekeeping" services. If the examples are extended to law-enforcement, city-planning and tax policy, for example, the argument that municipal government is "nonpolitical" becomes even less defensible.

There should be an end then to the argument that the character of local government frees it from the need for active and vigorous politics. The city differs only in degree from state and national government in its emphasis on nonpolicy considerations, and it is not always clear in which direction the difference lies, particularly when cities of several hundred thousand or millions of people are affected.

The political character of city government does not necessarily lead, however, to the easy possibility, much less the necessity in any city, of the *formalized* politics suggested by the partisan ballot. The evidence of this study has repeatedly demonstrated that the local election process tends to focus on personalities much more than on issues. This emphasis appears to be inherent in the nature of local government and perhaps especially so under the council-manager form. Politics oriented toward personalities are not peculiar to local government, of course, and recent history is replete with examples of state and national elections markedly shaped by personality considerations. The extent to which this is true at the municipal level, however, together with the relatively low stakes in terms of patronage and spoils, characteristic of California cities at least, affect the possibility of consistent formalized group competition, partisan or otherwise. In a community where basic issues continue to divide the citizenry or where the stakes of public office are sufficiently important to support a continuing political organization, the situation may be different.

2. *Accepting the view that there are political issues at the local level, questions that arise in local politics are irrelevant to issues which divide the national parties. Party interest, therefore, tends to be artificial, and the nonpartisan ballot is to be desired because it reduces the influence of party.*

Admitting that partisan positions and differences at the state or national level are not always readily discernible, the evidence of this study would, with few exceptions, support the first sentence

of this position of the nonpartisan advocates. Rarely in California
have municipal questions arisen on which a party position existed.
Of the six cities, only Berkeley was divided over public policy
which one could readily identify as partisan. In that city, controversy over public housing and the use of the school auditorium
resulted on two occasions in what might be classed as partisan
divisions, but these issues were both short-lived, and party positions were mixed. In the remaining five cities and in the responses
to the questionnaires, vice, the council-manager plan, parking
meters, annexation policy, and freeway location were typical of
the issues that had featured local election campaigns. In no election did the parties as such have an identifiable position on the
particular issues nor had they participated in the discussion concerning them, although in every election the questions had been
"hot." The one exception to this finding was in Pomona where the
Democratic club leadership had become active in a drive for re-
vision of the city charter but had incurred the active opposition
of many of the club's members.

Political parties can, of course, take opposite points of view on
city policies. For example, it is popularly held that Republicans
tend to be more "tax-conscious" and Democrats more "program
oriented" and this would be reflected in a variety of municipal
issues. However, the evidence of this study does not provide
strong support for even such a broad generalization. On few of
the burning community questions facing most California cities
is the pie cut into partisan pieces. To posit a regular and continuing natural kinship between party and local platform, therefore, does not seem to accord with the facts.

Implicit in the argument set forth above is the view that parties
are primarily "issue-oriented" and that the absence of a corres-
pondence between local and state-national issues reduces the
meaning of party activity in city affairs. But parties are often not
primarily interested in policy. "Partisan conflicts turn largely upon
questions of personnel and patronage." [2] The only reason cited
by the California Democratic Council Issues Conference, itself a
highly "issue-oriented" body, for increased party activity at the
local level was the fact that local offices "were offices in which
persons were being groomed for partisan office anyway, and that

---

[2] Odegard and Helms, *American Politics*, 2d ed., (1947), p. 204.

Republican vantage has been cloaked frequently in non-partisanship." [3] The need for and the desirability of party activity in local affairs cannot be judged solely on the basis of the party's issue orientation—which will probably be difficult to ascertain in any event—but must be evaluated by other criteria set forth below.

The nonpartisan ballot without doubt generally reduces the influence of party, although empirical support is lacking and directly conflicting evidence may be offered, e.g., Boston, Chicago, and Kansas City. The absence of official party activity reported in this study suggests that the removal of the party label tends to reduce the stake of the party organization and leaders in the outcome of the local races, and their interest and activity is correspondingly lessened. Adrian concludes on the basis of a general overview: "In most non-partisan elections, organizations identified with the major parties are of little or no importance in determining the outcome." [4]

Also, it is unquestionably true that the lack of a party designation on the ballot affects voter attitudes toward the election. The radical change in voting behavior in California primary elections following the addition of the party label in 1954 indicates this dramatically. Whether the shift was caused by voter awareness for the first time of the candidates' party affiliations, as is commonly suspected, or, whether, as Pitchell asserts, the labeling merely "changed the nature of the candidates' appeals and the voters' perceptions of the primary election," [5] the addition of the party label did alter existing relationships.

---

[3] California Democratic Council, *CDC Issues Conference, Election Reform Summary Report* (March, 1959), p. 3.

[4] Adrian, "A Typology for Nonpartisan Elections," *Western Political Quarterly,* XII (June, 1959), 458. However, Freeman concludes that "institutional devices are not likely to abolish a local two-party system in a city where attitudes toward the two major national parties are strongly structured and the relations between national and local party organizations are durable and persistent." "Local Party Systems: Theoretical Considerations and a Case Analysis," *The American Journal of Sociology,* LXIV (November, 1958), 289.

[5] Pitchell, "The Electoral System and Voting Behavior: The Case of California's Cross-Filing," *Western Political Quarterly,* XII (June, 1959), 480.

A sampling of Denver citizens before an important mayoralty race resulted in a finding somewhat in contrast to the views set forth here. There, similar panels differed only in that for the first group no mention was made of the candidate's party affiliation. In the material shown to the second panel, however, the party label was printed clearly above each candidate's picture. The survey showed that "even if the party affiliation of the candidates became generally known, this did not change the outcome, since when we showed the voters to which party each candidate belonged, the results for all practical purposes were identical with

3. *The evils of the machine, the boss, and the spoils system require that all "good citizens," irrespective of party, combine in the interests of good government, and the nonpartisan ballot promotes this and the strength of independent civic associations.*

Whatever the truth of the first half of this argument may have been at the turn of the century, it had little relevance to California in 1960. The absence of patronage, the improvement of fiscal, auditing, and management techniques and the extension of the city-manager plan in the state and the generally high professional standards associated with it are examples of built-in brakes against a return to the days of a Boss Ruef. Local graft and corruption have not completely disappeared, but the isolated examples have no ascertainable connection with party politics.

California's state administration, under more direct partisan influences, also meets the description of clean and honest government. Here, too, the few instances of malfeasance which will undoubtedly always occur have not been related to machines, bosses, or party patronage. In fact, it is a common assertion among observers in the state that the scandals which surrounded certain lobbyists and legislators in the state capitol in the early 1950's resulted from the weakness of the political parties, not their strength. This argument runs to the effect that pressure groups moved in to fill the vacuum created by the absence of vigorous party leadership and organization.

California provides an example, then, of a state in which the parties will have to prove their worth and the importance of their role without many of the traditional emoluments and spoils normally associated with partisan success. It also provides a context in which discussion over nonpartisanship at the local level can proceed unencumbered by the side issues of bosses, machines, and party patronage.

Perhaps for these reasons, among others, the independent civic associations envisaged by the early reformers have not generally continued active. American municipal history is replete with ex-

---

those found when the voters were not told the party affiliation of the candidates." Pearson, "Predictions in a Non-Partisan Election," *Public Opinion Quarterly,* XII (Spring, 1948), 112–117. On the basis of both the Pitchell and the Pearson conclusions, it might be hypothesized that party labeling does not necessarily alter voter knowledge or preference but that it does change the character of the election and voter attitudes regarding the meaning of the election.

amples of such organizations arising to meet a specific need, to oust a machine, or to sponsor some particular reform, and then withering once the problem has been resolved. While, in theory a nonpartisan system may make it more possible for independent groups to become active, the record makes it clear that they are difficult to maintain in the absence of specific needs for reform.

4. *Political parties will never be meaningful and useful instruments on the state and national scene as long as they must concern themselves with the minutiae of local government and be subject to the temptation of local spoils and patronage.*

The view is not an argument for nonpartisanship at the local level, particularly, but for strong partisanship at the right level. Schattschneider's views are typical of this concern. He argues for "a more powerful national party able to deny to the local boss all access to national patronage. . . . With the destruction of the boss system, the disastrous nexus of national and local politics, which depends on the boss for its survival, will collapse. Therefore it may be anticipated that municipal elections will be permitted to become purely local affairs." [6] The National Municipal League writes that the intervention of the national parties in municipal affairs "injects irrelevant considerations of local patronage and personal ambition into the national party counsels and thus tends to depreciate both the integrity and the clarity of national politics." [7]

It is difficult to determine the extent to which Schattschneider's views are tied to the problem of spoils and whether in the general absence of patronage, as in California, he would support the argument with the same fervor. Elsewhere in the same book, he appears to deny the possibility of separating local from state and national politics: "Political organizations are incurably multifunctional. Once a political army able to carry a municipal elec-

---

[6] Schattschneider, *Party Government* (1942), pp. 182–183.

[7] National Municipal League, *Getting the National Parties Out of Municipal Elections* (July, 1953), p. 1. As noted on page 37, the Cleveland Metro study group approached the problem from a contrasting point of view, concluding that it was desirable, if not essential, to introduce the parties into the local political scene. This was necessary, the committee stated, to provide some unifying force to "integrate the wide-ranging interest groups and to establish the basic lines of political argument for the voters." Partisan competition for the Metro executive "can serve to stimulate the energy and community consciousness of the two political parties." *Government Organization for Metropolitan Cleveland* (Report to the Cleveland Metropolitan Services Commission, 1959), pp. 7–9.

tion has been created, who is going to forbid its advantageous use in state and national elections also?"[8] In any event, the two political parties *are* locally based, bosses and machines or not, and there seems little evidence to support the view that they are becoming more centralized. The extension of the nonpartisan local ballot, as such, would appear to have little to do with increasing "the integrity and the clarity of national politics."

Thus, the question whether local political activity will, on the one hand, be "good exercise," strengthening the organization for its role in state and national politics, or will rather tend to fractionization and dissipation of organization energy does not permit generalization. The examples of Democratic party involvement in Chico and Berkeley have probably tended to increase the effectiveness of the party as an instrument in the partisan arena. In Pomona, however, a different involvement by a Democratic club, resulted in seriously damaging the existing organization, at least temporarily. Recent California history makes it clear that parties can be strengthened without engaging heavily in local elections, but this is not to meet the question directly.[9]

Nor will the answer necessarily be the same for the two parties. If the impressions of this study are correct, the Republican party has more of a "natural" organizational base than the Democrats

---

[8] Schattschneider, *op. cit.*, p. 149.

[9] In 1954, Farrelly and Fox made the statement concerning California: "It is virtually impossible to build an enduring precinct organization without the foundation of local campaigns. The killing of partisan spirit in municipal elections and the resultant weakening of party machinery means that the Democrats are precluded from mobilizing the vast voting potential found in their registration majority." See "Capricious California; A Democratic Dilemma," *Frontier*, VI (November, 1954), 6.

The fact that, although "handicapped" by the system of nonpartisan elections, the Democratic club movement in California has experienced rapid growth and has been active in apparently effective precinct work in state and national, but *not* municipal, elections suggests that such a conclusion requires further attention and cannot be accepted at face value. Party officials themselves do not necessarily favor participation in local politics. At a meeting of a county central committee in 1959 at which this topic was discussed, the writer heard the following arguments presented against party activity in city and county races: (1) It doesn't work from a practical standpoint, and the press will "crucify" you. (2) It drains campaign contributions away from partisan races. (3) It tends to produce splits in the party organization. (4) It dilutes the energies of the organization. (5) It dissipates the use and importance of the party name. (6) It ties partisan candidates at a state and national level to an army of local candidates of varying quality. (7) It embarrasses the party organization in that local candidates expect and demand support which they don't really deserve. Without debating the relative merits of these several points, they do constitute problems for politicians.

because of the dominance of Republican members in many community organizations and in local government itself. Thus, there may be less impetus for the Republicans than for the Democrats to develop a formal local political organization or to take part, as a party, in local elections.

5. *Better candidates can be recruited for local office if they do not have to fight their way through the party machine to get there; members of the national party which is in a minority in the city can still play their full role as participating citizens, and the city will be protected in its dealings with state and national officials because nonpartisan councils "commonly" have members of both parties within their membership.*[10]

This argument had great relevance in an earlier day under a system in which candidates for local office were nominated at party conventions, themselves inadequately insulated against the machinations of the boss. But today, the question remains equally important: does the nonpartisan system broaden and improve the base of those elected to public office? The evidence of this study is limited, but these facts are clear. The recruitment of able candidates is a serious problem in almost every California community. The political parties are now free to recruit and support candidates under the nonpartisan system, and they do. They would undoubtedly feel a greater necessity and responsibility to do so under a partisan ballot. On the other hand, placement of the party label on the ballot and increasing the partisan character of elections would certainly reduce the willingness of many persons to seek local office.

But are better candidates elected under the nonpartisan system? The question defies analysis, but one fact stressed in the previous chapter is clear: If "better" can be defined to include "representative" as one of its components the nonpartisan election system is seriously deficient. Here the problem is not that posed by the original nonpartisan advocates—the desirability of a system which would permit members of a minority political party to serve their community. The evidence of this study is persuasive

---

[10] The assertion that nonpartisan councils "commonly" contain both Republicans and Democrats is made in the National Municipal League's *Getting the National Parties Out of Municipal Elections* (July, 1953), p. 2.

that, in terms of membership, the minority party has the lion's share of local political offices in California.[11]

The problem is the representation of minorities—not of political parties but of social, racial, religious, and economic groups in the community to the extent that every citizen feels an identity with and a confidence in the actions of the city council, school board, or other local bodies.

This is not just a problem for nonpartisan communities alone. That the form of ballot is at most tangential to its solution is no doubt true. In fact, of the several progressive "reforms," the question of the ward versus at-large method of representation may be more crucial in this connection than the issue of the party label. In any event, it is certain that the situation can be improved, regardless of the election system.

6. *The extension of legal home rule reduces the need for city-state political ties and makes the possibility of "political home rule" more feasible. In any event, intergovernmental relations are carried on at the professional, not the party level.*

Goodnow, throughout his writing, repeatedly stressed the notion that partisan involvement in local affairs sprang in part from the fact that municipal governments were agents of the state. He urged a greater emphasis on administrative supervision and a corresponding decrease in legislative interference.[12] To a considerable degree, nonpartisan advocates were also vigorous in their support of home rule.

Without denying the relevance of this position at the turn of the century, it does not seem to contribute much to an understanding of the problem in 1960. Home rule, and it is vigorous in California, is carried on within a network of intergovernmental relationships, both legislative and administrative, far beyond those which Goodnow could perceive in 1897. It is true in California, however, that city-state relationships have little to do with party differences. Overt political interference by the state in the activities of California cities is practically unknown, and the question of the acceptance and the extent of home rule would appear to have little relationship to party politics. The absence

---

[11] In 1959, for example, fourteen (about one-fifth) of the cities in Los Angeles County had no Democratic council members at all, and another fourteen had only one Democratic legislator. Only nine cities had fewer than two Republican councilmen.

[12] Goodnow, *Municipal Problems* (1897), pp. 199–201.

of a division in California between an "up-state party" and a "down-state party" or a rural and city party is unquestionably critical in this connection. This is not, of course, a universal pattern across the nation.

7. *Parties are unable to promote group responsibility for candidates and programs in the city hall. Responsibility becomes possible when attention can be focused on local issues and programs as it can under the nonpartisan system.*

No one knows whether under a partisan form of local government a greater sense of collegial responsibility among city councilmen exists than under the nonpartisan system. It would seem likely that party is only one of several factors to influence responsibility. The same generalization would seem realistic with respect to the accountability of local officials to the voter. This study indicates the ability of the public to relate issues to candidates and vote accordingly when heated controversies arise, but there is no evidence to indicate whether this would be more or less possible and frequent under a partisan system. Key observes: "The proposition that an institutionalized collective leadership will on the average better promote the public weal than an atomized leadership of individuals must be in high degree an affirmation of faith rather than the confident utterance of a prediction." [13]

An appraisal of this argument is beyond our current knowledge. Nor can meaningful comparisons be made with the state or federal legislative bodies, because city councils are too different in their size, procedure, and substantive considerations.

8. *Nonpartisan elections are possible because, assuming a short ballot, "the voter can accumulate and carry in his head the brief list of personal preferences and do without the guidance of party names and symbols on the ballot."* [14]

This quotation of Richard Childs constitutes the heart of the nonpartisan approach. It typifies the description of Robert Wood that the nonpartisan advocate believes that "the individual can and should arrive at his political convictions untutored and unled." [15] For while Childs, for example, is willing to accept the fact that political groups and leaders can play a significant role, he decries the formation of blocs, of ticket-voting, of political

---

[13] Key, *American State Politics: An Introduction* (1956), p. 273
[14] Childs, *Civic Victories* (1952), p. 299.
[15] *Suburbia* (1958), p. 157.

organizations motivated by "power" as opposed to "civic" considerations. His reliance is on the ability of the individual voter to discern the worth of individual candidates.[16]

The evidence of this study concerning questions of voter motivation and behavior is especially limited. The findings do suggest, however, that the consideration of candidates and issues is frequently group-oriented, that the freeing of the voter from party ties may have as its concomitant an increased dependence on personality and nonparty considerations. Candidates may be "tied like bunches"—a Childs characterization of the results of the partisan election—regardless of the ballot form: by newspapers, by union endorsements, by social connections, and by a host of other factors. These ties may be as far from the rational, individual deliberation conceived by the nonpartisan advocate as would a "blind party vote."

Nonpartisanship, to be accurately appraised, then, must be set in the context—not of a highly rational electorate with perfect access to a wide body of information about local candidates and issues—but of average human beings with limited time and interest facing civic decisions amidst many conflicting and inevitably inadequate impressions, attitudes, and reports regarding public policies and officials.

In this "real world," the issue over the nonpartisan ballot does not turn on the existence of a "model citizen" but on whether

---

[16] The evidence of split-ticket voting revealed in an Indiana analysis is indicative of the ability of the electorate to look at individual candidates even under the partisan system. The report of local elections in 1947 stressed these three points: (1) split-ticket voting was widespread; (2) local issues often transcended partisan considerations in importance; (3) the election frequently featured a contest between competing groups within the same party, generally the machine versus a reform group, or between the local and state party organizations. "It may be concluded," said the author, "that split-ticket voting has elected so many mixed party administrations that it is clear that party labels had little effect on voting behavior in the majority of the cities surveyed." Wheeler, *Indiana Local Elections*, (1947–1948), p. 7.

Relevant also is the observation of the Lynds that the role of the party in the community has undergone change in our time: "The damping down almost to extinction of this flaming party ardor as one turns from national politics to Middletown's election of its own local officials is a social phenomena that will bear watching. . . . Not only does this represent a change from the Middletown of the 1880's, when a man who was a Republican or Democrat nationally tended to stand staunchly by the same party locally, but it also probably suggests the presence of a profound social change in process in the meaning of political symbols to Middletown." From *Middletown in Transition* by Robert S. Lynd & Helen Merrell Lynd, copyright, 1937, by Harcourt, Brace and Co.

among all the conflicting pressures, groups, and associations in the community, the public welfare would be best served by giving to the political party the preferential treatment of a place on the ballot.

This then is the question. Its answer rests not on any attempt to "depoliticize" the city by claiming its problems are merely "housekeeping." Nor on any hypothetical divorce of local from state and national issues. Nor, at least in California, on a concern over the spoils and machine politics of a by-gone age, either with respect to their impact on the city or the parties themselves.

Rather, we return to the basic issue of which system will do most to enhance the twin factors of competition and consensus essential to the democratic process. Which system will best promote freedom and equality of access to public office and political activity by all groups in the community? Which system will best encourage the presentation of alternative viewpoints on key issues facing the community and relate these views to candidate choice? And finally, which system will best lead to the recruitment and election of those men and women of ability and integrity without whom the community will fail to reach its potential as a vital force in the life of its citizens?

In answering these questions, each community will have to examine its own problems, needs, and resources. Important and helpful as they are in raising the question for debate, the generalizations of both the partisan and nonpartisan advocates can never be an adequate substitution for thoughtful individual consideration. The size of the city, the character of its population, the quality of its civic institutions, the integrity of its press—these and countless other matters will determine which type of ballot and which kind of politics will result in the most vital political life for the community and for its citizenry. But politics there will be. "A free people must lead a political life. . . . For the democratic system assumes that we are all politicians. If we are dissatisfied with parts of our political performance, we have the corrective at hand. It lies not in less politics but more and of a higher standard." [17]

It is part of the genius of the American republic that the decisions on ballot and politics will be largely resolved on a prag-

---

[17] "Politics: An Essential of Democracy," *Kansas City Star*, February 2, 1958.

matic, city-by-city basis and not be laid down by ukase either from Washington or from the various state capitols. Such is the diversity of America and such are the varying needs and qualities of her several thousand cities, that in this area of political life, more than anywhere else, home rule is consistent with democracy.[18]

---

[18] Said the attorney-general of California: "We regard the desires of the electorate of a county or city, expressed through the local legislative body, as a particularly appropriate event upon which to condition the effectiveness in such county or city of any statute relating to the role played by political parties in the nomination and elections of the county or city officers." California, Attorney General, *Opinions* No. 55/184 (April 16, 1956), p. 16.

APPENDIXES

APPENDIX A

The Six Cities

THE SIX CITIES MADE THE SUBJECT OF INVESTIGATION DO
not represent a "cross-section" of the state's several hundred cities,
but do illustrate different aspects of the state's life. Proceeding
from north to south, the six cities had the following characteristics. (Population and other data are as of 1960, and therefore
differ in some instances from the figures prevailing during the
time of the field work, 1955–1956.)

Chico (population 15,000 in 1960) is situated on the east side
of the Sacramento Valley about one hundred miles north of
Sacramento. It is the major trading center for a large and rich
diversified farm area, with emphasis on rice and almonds and

also has substantial local industry based on wood and food processing. Although not the county seat, it is the largest and most important city of Butte County; it is the home of Chico State College.

The population of the city is homogenous, tending to be white and Protestant. Less than a hundred nonwhites were reported in the 1950 census. As do other California cities, Chico faces fringe-area growth; almost as many people live in the immediate environs of the city but outside the corporate limits as within the city proper. The rate of population increase in the county in recent years has been double that of the city. The city itself had a population of 9,000 in 1940 and 12,000 in 1950.

The registered voters of the city are fairly evenly split in their partisan registration, and during the past years the city has given its vote to candidates of both parties. However, there has been a marked Republican preference for both national and state officers. The city is represented by a Republican assemblyman and state senator and by a Democratic congressman.

Chico has a council-manager government, long established by a home-rule charter. A council of five, all elected at large, serve four-years terms; the mayor is selected by the council from among its own membership; there are the usual number of appointive advisory commissions. Chico has an exceptionally large park area (Bidwell Park, 2,400 acres, is locally described as the second-largest municipal park in the United States) and a municipally owned airport.

Berkeley (population 110,000 in 1960), is situated on the east side of San Francisco Bay in Alameda County. Hemmed in geographically by the bay in the west and politically by the county line in the east, its population declined in the 1950's by 4,000 in contrast to the rapid growth of other California cities. Significant, however, have been the internal shifts which have recently taken place in the racial character of the city's population. From 4 per cent of the total population in 1940, the Negro community increased to an estimated 20 to 25 per cent of the 1960 population.

The city, part of the metropolitan complex of the Bay Area, is essentially a residential and university community with limited commercial and industrial development. It is the location of the main campus and state-wide administration of the University of

California, six divinity schools, and the state schools for the blind and the deaf.

Politically, the city is fairly evenly divided between the two parties in its registration, but the Democratic proportion has been slowly increasing in recent years. This is related to the growth of the Negro community, which is heavily Democractic. In state and national elections since the war, the city has tended to vote Republican, with the exception of the 1954 gubernatorial race and the 1958 Democratic sweep. Berkeley's registered Democrats actually vote Democratic in larger numbers than is generally true in the state. The city is represented by two assemblymen, a Republican and a Democrat (the latter one of two Negroes in the lower house), and by a Democratic congressman elected in 1958, replacing a long-time G.O.P. incumbent.

Berkeley is governed under a council-manager charter adopted in 1923. It provides for a separately elected mayor, chosen every four years, and a council of eight, all elected at large. An elected auditor is the only other elected municipal official. The city manager appoints the entire slate of administrative officers.

San Leandro (population 66,000 in 1960) lies eleven miles to the south of Berkeley, also on the east side of San Francisco Bay. Once primarily an agricultural town, it had by 1940 become a residential suburb (with a population of 15,000) that served largely as a bedroom community for nearby Oakland. War-time and postwar growth changed the character of the city completely. It is the center of southern Alameda County's mushrooming industrial development. The area of the city, in contrast to Berkeley, increased by approximately 500 per cent from 1940 to 1960.

The city's population is almost entirely Caucasian; there are important Portuguese and Italian colonies in San Leandro, most of whom are long-time residents and almost entirely Catholic.

The city's registered voters are more Democratic (66 per cent) than the county as a whole (62 per cent), both figures reflecting a sizeable increase in Democratic strength over the period of the 1950's. However, this preference has not carried over into voting for state-wide or national candidates. Following World War II the city voted consistently Republican until 1958. However, San Leandro is represented by a Democratic assemblyman and a Democratic congressman.

The city is governed under the council-manager form first installed under a home-rule charter in 1927 and included in the more recent charter adopted in 1949. A council of seven men, all of whom are elected at large, serve four-year terms and select the mayor from their own membership. The city is divided into six councilman districts, however, and each of the councilmen, save one, must reside in and be nominated (by petition) from his own separate district.

Fresno (population 133,000 in 1960) is the largest and most important city of the San Joaquin Valley, one of the richest farming regions in the nation. Fresno County frequently leads the country in the total value of its agricultural production, and the economy of the city centers on the production, processing, and marketing of grapes, raisins, wine, cotton, barley, alfalfa, and beef cattle. Fresno has more than doubled its population since 1940, and this growth has been accompanied by substantial annexations which have added one-third to the city's size in recent years.

Fresno is noted for the heterogeneity of its population. The 1950 census reported 10,000 foreign-born white and 7,000 non-white out of a total of 92,000, but these figures do not reveal the presence in the community of many foreign-language groups of native-born Americans, including substantial numbers of citizens of Mexican, Armenian, German, Volga German, Italian, Yugoslav, and Greek descent.

Both Fresno city and county have a two-to-one Democratic registration as compared with the three-to-two margin in the state as a whole. Since World War II, the city has tended to vote for Democratic presidential candidates, while its vote for state-wide candidates has been mixed. Currently the city is represented by two Democratic assemblymen, a Democratic state senator, and a Democratic congressman. Before 1958, a Republican had held one of the Assembly seats.

Fresno was the last city in the state to retain the commission form of government. The commission was composed of three full-time "administrative" and four part-time "legislative" commissioners, all elected at large for four-year terms. The commissioner of public safety was also the city's mayor. The city adopted a council and administrative-officer charter in 1957.

Unlike the other five cities, Fresno's recent municipal history has been characterized by a struggle over commercialized vice, and knowledge of the uncertainty and disagreement in the city over the present closed-town policy is essential to an understanding of local politics.

Pomona (population 67,000 in 1960) is situated twenty-eight miles east of downtown Los Angeles. Part of a huge metropolitan region, it constitutes in its own right a central position as the trading center for eastern Los Angeles County and has a substantial business section serving the city and the outlying area. Population growth within the city has been typical of the area as a whole— a more than 150 per cent increase from 1940 to 1960. Unlike many other communities, Pomona's growth has taken place largely within existing city territory, a phenomenon made possible by the existence of large agricultural areas, principally in citrus, within city boundaries. The city is primarily a residential community but has a substantial industrial area.

The population in 1950 was 99 per cent white and 93 per cent American-born. The city, regarded as a "strong church town," is 75 per cent Protestant and has a large Mexican-American population most of whom are Catholics.

In its political registration, the city is about evenly split between the two major parties, whereas the county registration is three-to-two Democratic. The voting habits of the citizenry are strongly Republican, however, and Eisenhower carried the city by two-to-one in 1952. The city voted for Democrat Brown in 1958, albeit by a narrow (53 per cent) margin.

Pomona is governed under a charter adopted in 1911, which provides for a separately elected mayor with a two-year term and four councilmen who serve four-year terms. Although the latter group is elected at large, they must each reside in and be nominated by a petition of residents of a separate ward of the city. A city clerk, city treasurer, and city attorney are also separately elected. The city is administered under terms of an ordinance establishing an administrative officer, who, in fact, has most of the powers and responsibilities of a city manager. Attempts to adopt a council-manager charter have not yet proven successful.

Maywood (population 15,000 in 1960), is one of the smallest cities of the state in terms of area. Situated in the heart of metropolitan Los Angeles, it comprises only one hundred and forty blocks. Surrounded by industry, the city itself is primarily a residential community of small, middle-income, single-family and two-story apartment houses. There is a limited commercial area, consisting primarily of small retail establishments, used-car lots and real-estate offices.

The population of the city is almost entirely Caucasian, a 1953 special census listing only three nonwhites. The city gained only slightly in population between 1950 and 1960, an indication that it has reached a saturation of population. A substantial number of Mormons live in Maywood.

Unlike any of the other cities visited, Maywood is not truly a community in the common sense of the term. It has few schools, churches, or social organizations of its own but shares such institutions with neighboring cities which surround it on three sides. These facts and the small size of the city minimize the importance of political statistics, which indicate that the city is registered two-thirds Democratic but is closely divided in its actual voting preferences for national or state-wide candidates.

Maywood is the only noncharter city of the six and is governed under general state law which provides for a five-man council, elected for four-year terms, which selects a mayor from its own members. Also elected are the city clerk and a part-time treasurer. Many city services are provided by the county under contract, and other functions are handled by special districts and by private contract. Police, fire, street maintenance, planning, and recreation constitute the main functions of the municipality.

APPENDIX B

The Opinion and Attitude Survey of California Civic Leaders

THE DISTRIBUTION OF QUESTIONNAIRES AMONG CIVIC leaders and political observers in the state and the responses received were discussed on page 43. Tables were presented indicating the distribution of the replies from city respondents according to the population of the city and the form of government.

Included in this appendix are tables showing the distribution of the replies to the city and county questionnaires by type of respondent and the replies to the county-chairmen questionnaire by county population and political affiliation of the chairmen. The two questionnaires are likewise included.

TABLE 54

WHO REPLIED TO THE QUESTIONNAIRE?

Respondent	Number mailed	Number returned	Per cent returned
City respondents	602	265	44
Mayors	*315*	*100*	*32*
City managers, chief administrative officers, etc	*167*	*119*	*71*
Editors, publishers, other newspapermen	*120*	*46*	*38*
County political chairmen	116	58	50
TOTAL	718	323	45

TABLE 55

REPLIES TO COUNTY POLITICAL CHAIRMEN QUESTIONNAIRE

	Counties			Chairmen				
						Replies		
County population	Total	Replies	Per cent replies	Total	Repub- licans	Demo- crats	Total	Per cent
Less than 5,000	3	2	67	6	2	1	3	50
5,000-10,000	3	2	67	6	1	1	2	33
10,000-25,000	14	10	71	28	8	6	14	50
25,000-50,000	6	5	83	12	2	3	5	42
50,000-100,000	10	8	80	20	6	7	13	65
100,000-250,000	10	9	90	20	4	5	9	45
250,000-500,000	8	7	88	16	4	7	11	69
500,000-1,000,000	3	1	33	6	1	0	1	17
More than 1,000,000	1	0	0	2	0	0	0	0
TOTAL	58	44	76	116	28	30	58	50

QUESTIONNAIRE SENT TO MAYORS, CITY MANAGERS AND EDITORS

346 Library Annex

University of California

Berkeley 4, California

LOCAL ELECTIONS QUESTIONNAIRE

1. If someone wished to run for election to your city council, the support (public or behind-the-scenes) of which of the following persons or groups would be most helpful to his success:

a. Please indicate first, second, third, etc. in importance by placing number 1, 2, 3, etc, in bracket. Indicate as many groups as needed to describe your local situation.

Realtors .... ( )	Improvement associations .... ( )
Merchants .... ( )	Women's organizations .... ( )
Bankers .... ( )	Veterans groups .... ( )
Teachers .... ( )	Political party organizations .. ( )
Attorneys .... ( )	Service clubs .... ( )
Ministers .... ( )	Masonic lodge .... ( )
Contractors .... ( )	Other lodges .... ( )
Manufacturers ...... ( )	Labor unions .... ( )
Liquor dealers,	Lay church groups .... ( )
bartenders ...... ( )	Local newspaper .... ( )
City employees .... ( )	Public utilities .... ( )
Doctors, dentists .. ( )	

Other (please list) _____

b. If there are any groups in the above list whose *public* support would *hurt* a candidate's chances, please indicate each of these in the above brackets with an X.
Other (please list) _____

2. Are there in your city any *organized* groups, such as a civic league, good government association, or labor union, that regularly put forward or endorse city council candidates, prepare and circulate campaign literature, or engage in similar public political activities:
YES ( )   NO ( )
If YES,
GROUP 1
a. What is the name of the group:_____
b. From what groups in the city (merchants, union labor, veterans, etc.) do the members come:_____
c. Are the candidates of this group successful:
     Frequently ( )   Sometimes ( )   Rarely ( )

GROUP 2
a. What is the name of the group:_____
b. From what groups in the city (merchants, union labor, veterans, etc.) do the members come:_____
c. Are the candidates of this group successful:
     Frequently ( )   Sometimes ( )   Rarely ( )
(Please list below if more than two groups.)

3. Are there in your city any *informal* groups of citizens that *regularly* get together before each city election to recruit candidates, donate

money for campaigning, provide personal support, or the like:
YES ( )   NO ( )

If YES,

GROUP 1

a. From what groups in the city (merchants, union labor, veterans, etc.) do the members come :_____

b. Are the candidates of this group successful:
   Frequently ( )   Sometimes ( )   Rarely ( )

GROUP 2

a. From what groups in the city (merchants, union labor, veterans, etc.) do the members come:_____

b. Are the candidates of this group successful:
   Frequently ( )   Sometimes ( )   Rarely ( )

(Please list below if more than two groups.)

4. Do incumbents on the council generally play an important role in *recruiting* new candidates for council office:
   YES ( )   NO ( )

5. Do candidates generally run as individuals, as part of a slate, or do they do both:
   Individual ( )   Slate ( )   Both ( )

6. Would you estimate the range of cost of a typical successful campaign:
   For mayor $_____ For council $_____

7. Does the local press support or endorse candidates for *city* office:
   Every election( ) Many elections( ) Few elections( ) Never( )
   Do candidates supported by the press generally win:
   Always( )   Many times( )   Occasionally( )   Never( )

8. In the last election campaigns for mayor and/or council, have the races been decided more on the basis of issues or on the basis of personalities:
   Issues( )   Personalities( )
   If Issues, what were they. (Please list.)_____

9. Do you have any reason to believe that the members of any groups or people living in particular areas in your city tend to vote together for the same candidates in *city* elections. (Please check any such group.)

Don't know .... ( )	Members of the same religion .. ( )
Well-to-do residen-	Racial minorities .... ( )
tial sections .... ( )	Business community .... ( )
Lower income resi-	Republicans .... ( )
dential sections .. ( )	Democrats .... ( )
New subdivisions	
or tracts .... ( )	
Old-timers .... ( )	
National or foreign	
language groups .. ( )	
Other (please list)_____	

---

10. In any election for *city* or *school* office in your city in the last *four* years, has there been any *public or openly visible activity* on the part of either political party organization: county committee, local political clubs, party officials or representatives, etc.:

    YES ( )   NO ( )

    If YES,

    a. What city or school elections have been involved:

        Mayor( )   City Council( )   School Board( )

    b. What sorts of activities have been involved. (Please check as many activities for each party as needed to describe the situation in your city.)

	By Reps.	By Dems.
Public endorsement of candidates	( )	( )
Use of party precinct machinery	( )	( )
Use of funds and/or fund raising	( )	( )
Use of party offices as headquarters	( )	( )
Other activities (please indicate which party)_____		

---

    c. In your opinion, did this party activity help the candidates:

       Helped( )   Made no difference( )   Hurt( )

11. In contrast with political party *organizations,* are individual party *leaders* in your city (county committeemen, party campaign chairmen or club officers, and others influential and active in party affairs) also active in elections for *city* office, either as partisans or nonpartisans. (Please check appropriate answer for each party.)

Leading Republicans	*Leading Democrats*
Many are active in	Many are active in
city elections ( )	city elections ( )
Some are active in	Some are active in
city elections ( )	city elections ( )

Few are active in   Few are active in
  city elections ( )   city elections   ( )
None are active in   None are active in
  city elections ( )   city elections   ( )

12. In the last *ten* years, as best as you can remember, has any local
    official (city, county, or school) or ex-local official run for state or
    national office in your area:

    YES ( )   NO ( )

	1st Candidate	2nd Candidate	3rd Candidate
If YES,			
a. What local office did he hold:	_____	_____	_____
b. What state or national office did he seek:	_____	_____	_____
c. Was he successful:	Yes( ) No( )	Yes( ) No( )	Yes( ) No( )

    (Please list below if more than three candidates)

13. Finally, if you would care to give your opinion, would you favor
    a state or city law requiring that the political affiliation, if any, of
    candidates for *city* office be entered on the city election ballot fol-
    lowing the candidate's name:
       YES ( )   NO ( )

On the reverse side, I would greatly appreciate your written comments
concerning groups involved in city elections and their activities; the
leadership the city election system produces in your area; problems, if
any, arising out of the system; and any other information that would
help me better to understand your local situation. Thank you.

_____
Name   Title

_____
City

QUESTIONNAIRE SENT TO
COUNTY POLITICAL CHAIRMEN

346 Library Annex
University of California
Berkeley 4, California

LOCAL ELECTIONS QUESTIONNAIRE

1. In any election for *city, county,* or *school office* (*not* state or national office) in your county in the last four years, has there been any *public or openly visible* activity on the part of either political party organization: county committee, local political clubs, party officials or representatives, etc.:
   YES ( )   NO ( )
   If YES,
   a. What county elections, if any, have been involved:
      District Attorney ( )   Sheriff ( )   Supervisor ( )
      Other (please list)_____
   b. What city or school elections, if any, have been involved:
      Mayor ( )   Council ( )   School Board ( )
      Other (please list)_____
   c. What sorts of activities have been involved. (Please check as many activities for each party as needed to describe the situation in your county.)

	,By Reps.	By Dems.
Public endorsement of candidates	( )	( )
Use of party precinct machinery	( )	( )
Use of funds and/or fund raising	( )	( )
Use of party offices as headquarters		
Other activities (please indicate which party)_____		

2. In contrast with political party *organizations,* are individual party *leaders* in your area (county committeemen, party campaign chairmen or club officers, and others influential and active in party affairs) also active in elections for *city, county,* or *school* office, either as partisans or nonpartisans. (Please check appropriate answers for each party.)

	In City Elections	*In County Elections*	*In School Board Elections*
Leading Republicans:			
Many are active	( )	( )	( )
Some are active	( )	( )	( )
Few are active	( )	( )	( )
None are active	( )	( )	( )
Leading Democrats:			
Many are active	( )	( )	( )
Some are active	( )	( )	( )
Few are active	( )	( )	( )
None are active	( )	( )	( )

3. As county chairman, have you or your predecessor *in the past four years* looked to the ranks of city, county, or school office-holders to seek candidates for state or national office:

Often ( )   Sometimes ( )   Never ( )

4. In the last *ten* years, as best as you can remember, has any local official (city, county, or school) or ex-local official actually run for state or national office in your area:

YES ( )   NO ( )

If YES,

	1st Candidate	*2nd Candidate*	*3rd Candidate*
a. What local office did he hold	_____	_____	_____
b. What state or national office did he seek	_____	_____	_____
c. Was he successful	Yes( ) No( )	Yes( ) No( )	Yes( ) No( )

(Please list below if more than three)

5. Finally, if you would care to give your opinion, would you favor a state or city law requring that the political affiliation, if any, of candidates for *city* office be entered on the city election ballot following the candidate's name:

YES ( )   NO ( )

Below or on a separate sheet, I would greatly appreciate your written comments concerning groups involved in local (city, county, or school) elections and their activities; the leadership the local election system produces in your area; problems, if any, arising out of the system; and any other information that would help me better to understand your local situation. Thank you.

_____

Name

Rep. ( )   Dem. ( )

_____

County   Party

BIBLIOGRAPHY

Selected Research

Current knowledge of local politics is fragmentary and incon-
clusive. What information does exist has neither been critically
inventoried nor thoughtfully integrated. In his bibliographical
essay, "Political Science and the Study of Urbanism," Robert
Daland observes: "While the total literature of municipal government is vast, the significant scholarly literature of urban government is small in amount and limited in coverage." Specifically,
Daland notes the paucity of material on urban politics, under-
lined by the fact that the chapter on politics in *Metropolitan
Communities: A Bibliography* covers only four pages of a total of
321.

The following listing is neither exhaustive in terms of the subjects included nor of the references cited. The works mentioned do, however, suggest the types of local political research which appear in the literature and which were of assistance in the development of this study. Complete citations follow in the bibliography.

GENERAL STUDIES

Much of the published information on local politics has been provided by sociologists. Three such studies concern the pseudonymous cities of Middletown, Plainville, and Yankee City, the work of the Lynds, Withers, and Warner and Lunt. In each, the political process is considered as but a part, albeit an important part, of the total stream of social forces under examination. The role of government in the life of the community, of political leaders in the social hierarchy, of differing groups in the political process are all considered. Only incidental attention is given to the electoral process as such.

Related to these are the "social or community profile" studies, best and most ambitiously represented by *The Detroit Area Study* of Michigan University, aimed at "depicting the social characteristics of the area by methods of modern social science." A less sophisticated series, typical of many with a community-welfare emphasis, is *Preparing a Community Profile* of the Bureau of Community Service of the University of Kentucky, based on community leader impressions in a number of cities and counties. Other university agencies active in this field include the University of Chicago with its "community inventory," the University of Wisconsin Bureau of Community Development, and the University of Nebraska Council for Community Study. Local welfare and planning studies have concerned themselves with similar problems. More general in approach have been accounts published by Agricultural Experiment Stations in several areas, of which the reports by W. A. Anderson on Waterville (New York) and by Beegle and Schroeder on the North Lansing (Michigan) fringe area are typical. All these provide helpful information on various phases of the community social scene. Some present specific but generally limited data on community leadership and political organization. Almost none mention the local electoral process.

In contrast to these studies of the "total" community, politics and government are given central emphasis in two recent works. The first, by Vidich and Bensman, examines "class, power and religion" in a small village in up-state New York, the second, by A. H. Birch, the political and administrative life of a British town of 20,000. Both concern themselves with the patterns of elected leadership and the character of the political process including the political parties and nonparty groups.

Robert Wood's *Surburbia,* on the other hand, attempts to describe the pattern of community affairs and politics, not in a single city, but in a *type* of community existing throughout the nation. In this ambitious endeavor, the author relies heavily on previously published material, attempting to synthesize existing sociological and political research into an understandable picture of suburban political life. He treats nonpartisanship as a prime characteristic of suburban behavior, not merely as a form of election.

Examples of the history of a single community are rare. A recent account by Theodore Brown of Kansas City's municipal government and its politics during the past quarter-century demonstrates how much the literature would be enriched by parallel studies of other cities.

COMMUNITY LEADERSHIP STUDIES

Interest in local power or leadership has produced studies of political scientists and sociologists. Floyd Hunter's, the most ambitious, attempts to discover the few persons in the community who really determine public policy. The formal role of politicians and elections is, however, virtually ignored. Robert K. Merton's more restricted study in *Communications Research* is a description of the "influentials" in the city of "Revere" in terms of various characteristics and attitudes. Politics as such, and more particularly the election process, are not subjects of direct concern.

In contrast to these, Robert Daland's *Dixie City* concentrates its attention on the formally designated political leaders of the community, their characteristics and their activities, and deliberately fails to touch upon the relationships of these persons "to the total power structure of Dixie City." Agger and Goldrich, on the other hand, in their study of two Oregon towns, examine "the nature of, and relationships between, the political parties in the community, the informal Republican organization of Main Street, and the local power structure."

Smuckler's and Belknap's *Leadership and Participation in Urban Political Affairs,* has as its major objective the presentation of "an inventory of the community from the standpoint of such characteristics as leadership pattern, group activity, and problem identification." The study uses polling techniques to obtain a picture in a single community of: (1) the leadership groups as seen by the group itself and by the general citizenry, and (2) the attitudes of these two groups concerning local, state, and national public problems.

Leadership studies have rarely investigated the local electoral process directly. One of the most complete accounts, although almost forty years old, is R. D. McKenzie's "attempt to discover and evaluate the more important of [the groups or forces which determine social and political policies] . . . as they have exhibited themselves in the municipal elections of Seattle during the thirteen years that the city has been under the system of nonpartisan elections." This analysis in the *Journal of Social Forces* considers the occupation and residential location of candidates and incumbents, the role of various groups in the election process, and the support given to candidates by various blocs of voters in the community. The author evaluates the change in the political process which occurred when the ballot was made nonpartisan.

PRESSURE GROUP STUDIES

Few works in the voluminous literature dealing with the role of pressure groups and special-interest organizations in politics consider their role at the local level. Municipal-government texts (for example, William Anderson's *American City Government*) rely on undocumented discussion, at times with considerable sophistication, but rarely include the activities of pressure groups in election campaigns. An examination of local politics as incidental to a more general inquiry is found in David Truman's

The Governmental Process. In dealing with active national political interests, he considers the role of the local party organization; but the local political process is not discussed.

Similar incidental discussion of group activity in local politics is found in Victor Jones's *Metropolitan Government,* which describes the interests lined up for and against various metropolitan integration proposals. This approach resembles that of the Stone, Price, and Stone series, in which each of the case studies of council-manager cities contains reference to those segments of the community which are active in supporting or opposing the manager plan.

The main work in this field is Meyerson's and Banfield's account of the decision-making process in planning public housing in Chicago. The authors give detailed attention to the role of pressure groups, politicians, and administrators in shaping the outcome of a struggle over the selection of sites for public housing. In so doing, the role of the partisan political machine in legally nonpartisan Chicago is sharply outlined.

POLITICAL-PARTY STUDIES

Abundant literature exists, of course, about the two-party system, discussing the role of the "organization" at the local level, the importance of the urban vote in national politics, and related topics. Generally speaking, however, scant attention is paid to the interrelationship of city and national politics.

With reference specifically to the political party structure, V. O. Key suggests in the *American Political Science Review* of June, 1953:

> The textbooks contain singularly little systematic analysis of the role of party in local government. They abstract the relevant statutes. They expound more or less orthodox suppositions. Voting on local candidates corresponds closely with presidential voting. Party groups compete for control of local government more or less as they do on the national level. Or, the contrary notion is argued that party has little place in local politics. Personal followings or essentially non-party courthouse cliques determine all.

In fact, as Key separately suggests, in *American State Politics,* students of American politics have neglected the study of politics of the *states* of the Union.

This paucity of research is balanced, in part, by several studies of city bosses and machines, such as the Gosnell and Merriam studies of Chicago. But most of these are now dated, if not obsolete, and generally their focus on the particular city is so sharp and the cities so unique as to make the studies not generally applicable.

Recent works include Ralph Straetz's study of politics and city government, *PR Politics in Cincinnati*, Robert Scigliano's unpublished thesis on Democratic party activities in Los Angeles, and Seymour Freedgood's popular review of big city political leadership in *The Exploding Metropolis*. Of these, Straetz's account is outstanding in its attempt to evaluate the impact of a unique election system upon the conduct of public affairs in a large city.

POLITICAL BEHAVIOR STUDIES

With the recent emphasis on the behavioral studies, works on political behavior" far exceed in number those in the preceding classifications. The works cited under this heading below are closely related, of course, to those discussed earlier, and their separate listing is one of convenience only.

National Studies of Political Behavior.—Exemplified in an earlier day by Arthur Holcombe's *The Political Parties of Today* in 1924, the past three decades have featured a series of studies attempting to explain the behavior of the American electorate in presidential balloting. Relying originally on historical and electoral data and more recently on public-opinion polling, the studies have included a sequel by Holcombe in 1933, Harold Gosnell's statistical study of 1942, Bean's *How to Predict Elections* in 1948, Lubell's two works of 1951 and 1956, and Louis Harris's 1954 account. All these emphasized the interplay, attitudes, and influences of groups and sections across the nation, but a second type of study, Angus Campbell's *The Voter Decides*, concentrated its attention on the voter's "perceptions" of the 1952 campaign. Using the same source of data, Alfred de Grazia in *The Western*

Public tested the allegation that the western United States was politically "unique."

None of these authors devotes special attention to the local political scene, although Gosnell in *Grass Roots Politics* predicts the future of urban politics as the national parties more frequently divide on economic class lines. All the studies, however, discuss the urban voter in the context of national politics and serve to provide a more meaningful picture of the setting in which local politics take place. In addition, the attitude studies of Campbell and DeGrazia concentrate on the psychology of the voting decision, a subject of inquiry with direct application to elections at all levels.

Community Studies of Political Behavior.—In addition to the mentioned studies based on nation-wide polling, there have been studies of the voting behavior of individual communities (Edward Litchfield, Edward Olds, Calvin Schmid, Robert Tryon). All these have attempted to relate political attitudes and electoral choices to demographic data such as race, religion, occupation, income level, sex, and extent of education. Mostly the political attitudes under study have been those concerned exclusively with national issues, candidates, or parties; in two instances, however, the St. Louis and Seattle studies by Olds and Schmid, respectively, data were gathered on local elections as well, and some attempt was made to investigate possible correlations between local, state, and national voting behavior.

The Lazersfeld and Berelson studies, in addition to investigating demographic relationships, analyze the development of the individual electoral decision during the campaign, the method employed being the repeated interviewing of a panel of respondents. The Erie County study in 1940 tended not to emphasize the pattern of community politics as a factor influencing political behavior, a shortcoming deliberately noted and overcome in the later Elmira report.

Community Studies of Political Participation.—Several studies on general political behavior consider voting participation and attempt to relate registration and turnout to some demographic characteristics. Charles Titus's original studies of California cities in the first quarter of this century explored the relationship between size of city and turnout. Roscoe Martin's study of the

Austin electorate and James Pollock's Ann Arbor analysis use demographic data in an attempt to describe the composition of the voters as compared with the public generally.

Robert Lane's *Political Life* is concerned with more than voter participation and offers as its subtitle, "Why People Get Involved in Politics." Its references to local politics are relatively infrequent, but the author does present hypotheses about the causes of low participation in municipal elections, including references to the nonpartisan ballot.

A recent study of metropolitan Detroit by Samuel Eldersveld focuses "on one major dimension of individual behavior, the degree of personal attachment to the political party" and on "the degree of involvement and participation in the party's work as a group." Participation at the polls is only one of the measurements used to assess political affiliation.

Different, but indicating how much the study of local politics would be advanced if a few basic records were centrally maintained, is Lawrence O'Rourke's *Voting Behavior in the Forty-Five Cities of Los Angeles County*. This helpful document reports the annual registration and total vote cast, in absolute and percentage figures, in state, national, and municipal elections for an eighteen-year period in each of the cities.

Miscellaneous.—Two valuable studies not falling into any of the above categories are V. O. Key's article on "Partisanship and County Office: The Case of Ohio" and John Wheeler's monograph, *Indiana Local Elections, 1947*. The first is an attempt to explore the relationship between Ohio voting behavior for presidential candidates and partisan county officials elected at the same time, and to discover the reasons for the differences. The second is an examination of the apparent split-ticket voting of the Indiana electorate in the 1947 municipal (partisan) elections. Both studies provide data in relatively unexplored territory.

Of a different character is Robert Lee's unpublished master's thesis, "The Berkeley Municipal Election of 1947," an example of a comprehensive analysis of a local election campaign. The Wichita municipal election of 1957 is described in Melvin Harder's *Nonpartisan Election*, one of the few published accounts of a local campaign. Another is Jack New's account of the partisan Bloomington municipal race of 1947 published by the University of Indiana Institute of Government. Arthur Bromage's brief description of his race for the city council is in a similar vein.

ANALYSES OF THE NONPARTISAN SYSTEM OF ELECTIONS

Several dissertations and articles have attempted to focus on the characteristics and implications of the nonpartisan system of balloting.

Charles Adrian's thesis "The Nonpartisan Legislature in Minnesota" concerned itself with the Minnesota legislature (one of the two elected under a nonpartisan ballot in the United States) and had as its purpose "not only to learn the methods used in the election of legislators without party labels, but also to examine the nature of the problems created by the absence of party organization and the attempted solution of those problems." In an article published by the *American Political Science Review* he broadened his focus to include two city councils as well as the Nebraska legislature and attempted to describe "Some General Characteristics of Nonpartisan Elections." Maurice Ramsey's dissertation is a general descriptive account of the Detroit city experience under the nonpartisan ballot and an attempt to explain what it has meant to that city.

Adrian has continued his analysis of local politics in an article in *The Western Political Quarterly* which classifies nonpartisan elections throughout the United States into four types, based partly on the role of the major party organizations. A second article, co-authored with Oliver Williams, discusses the relationships between partisan and nonpartisan voting patterns in four cities. A report by George Pearson of a Denver campaign presents the results of a sampling of public opinion in a nonpartisan race, attempting to show the absence of party interest in that particular contest. Finally, in an article in *The American Journal of Sociology*, J. Leiper Freeman sets forth a typology of local politics in terms of conventional concepts of one-, two-, and multiparty systems and, within this theoretical context, presents the results of a case study of a nonpartisan city.

Books, Theses, Reports, and Monographs

Adrian, Charles R. "The Nonpartisan Legislature in Minnesota." Unpublished doctoral dissertation, University of Minnesota, Milwaukee, 1950.

Albright, Spencer D. *The American Ballot*. Washington, D.C.: American Council on Public Affairs, 1942.

American Political Science Association. *Toward a More Responsible Two-Party System*. New York: Rinehart, 1950.

Anderson, W. A. *Social Change in a Central New York Rural Community*. (Bulletin no. 907.) Ithaca: Cornell University, Agricultural Experiment Station, 1954.

Anderson, William. *American City Government*. New York: Henry Holt, 1925.

Anderson, William, and Edward W. Weidner. *American City Govern-ment*. Rev. ed. New York: Henry Holt, 1950.

Angelo, Louis. "Party Reorganization and Election Reform in Cal-ifornia." Unpublished master's thesis, University of California, Berkeley, 1959.

Beegle, J. Allen, and Widick Schroeder, *Social Organization in the North Lansing Fringe*. (Technical Bulletin no 251.) East Lansing: Michigan State University, Agricultural Experiment Station, 1955.

Berelson, Bernard R., *et al., Voting*. Chicago: University of Chicago Press, 1954.

Birch, A. H. *Small-Town Politics: A Study of Political Life in Glossop*. London: Oxford University Press, 1959.

Bridenbaugh, Carl. *Cities in Revolt: Urban Life in America, 1743–1776*. New York: Alfred A. Knopf, 1955.

Bromage, Arthur. *Introduction to Municipal Government and Admin-istration*. New York: Appleton-Century-Crofts, 1950.

Brooks, Robert C. *Political Parties and Electoral Problems*. 3d ed., rev. New York: Harper, 1933.

Brown, A. Theodore. *The Politics of Reform: Kansas City's Municipal Government 1925–1950*. Kansas City, Missouri: Community Studies Inc., 1958.

Campbell, Angus, *et al., The Voter Decides*. Evanston, Illinois: Row, Peterson, 1954.

Childs, Richard S. *Civic Victories; The Story of an Unfinished Revolu-tion*. New York: Harper, 1952.

Cleveland Metropolitan Services Commission. *Government Organiza-tion for Metropolitan Cleveland*. Cleveland: Cleveland Metropolitan Services Commission, 1959.

Cresap, Dean R. *Party Politics in the Golden State*. Los Angeles: The Haynes Foundation, 1954.

Crouch, Winston W., *et al., California Government and Politics*. Engle-wood Cliffs, N.J.: Prentice-Hall, 1956.

———. *State and Local Government in California*. Berkeley and Los Angeles: University of California Press, 1952.

Daland, Robert T. *Dixie City: A Portrait of Political Leadership*. Uni-versity, Ala.: University of Alabama, Bureau of Public Administra-tion, 1956.

de Grazia, Alfred. *The Western Public; 1952 and Beyond*. Stanford: Stanford University Press, 1954.

Eldersveld, Samuel J. *Political Affiliation in Metropolitan Detroit*. Ann Arbor: University of Michigan, Institute of Public Administration, Bureau of Government, 1957.

Fisher, Marguerite J. and Edith E. Starrett. *Parties and Politics in the*

Local Community (Bulletin no. 20). Washington, D.C.: The National Council for the Social Studies, 1945.

Freedgood, Seymour. "New Strength in City Hall," *in The Exploding Metropolis,* by the editors of *Fortune* magazine. Garden City, N.Y.: Doubleday, 1958.

Goodnow, Frank J. *Municipal Problems.* New York: Macmillan, 1897.

Gosnell, Harold F. *Grass Roots Politics: National Voting Behavior of Typical States.* Washington, D.C.: American Council on Public Affairs, 1942.

———. *Machine Politics: Chicago Model.* Chicago: University of Chicago Press, 1937.

Gouldner, Alvin W., ed., *Studies in Leadership.* New York: Harper, 1950.

Government Affairs Foundation. *See* Victor Jones, *et al.*

Greenfield, Margaret. *Legislative Reapportionment: California in National Perspective* (Legislative Problem Series, 1959, no. 7). Berkeley: University of California, Bureau of Public Administration, 1959.

Greer, Scott. "Individual Participation in Mass Society," *in* Roland Young, ed., *Approaches to the Study of Politics.* Evanston: Northwestern University Press, 1958.

Griffiths, Ernest S. *The Modern Development of City Government in the United Kingdom and the United States.* London: Oxford University Press, 1927.

Harder, Melvin A. *Nonpartisan Election: A Political Illusion.* (Case Studies in Practical Politics.) New York: Henry Holt, 1958.

Harris, Joseph P. *California Politics.* Stanford: Stanford University Press, 1955.

———. *Election Administration in the United States.* Washington, D.C.: The Brookings Institution, 1934.

Harris, Joseph P., and Leonard Rowe. *California Politics.* 2d ed., rev. Stanford: Stanford University Press, 1959.

Harris, Louis. *Is There a Republican Majority?* New York: Harper, 1954.

Holcombe, Arthur N. *The New Party Politics.* New York: W.W. Norton, 1933.

———. *The Political Parties of Today.* New York: Harper, 1924.

Hollingshead, August B. *Elmtown's Youth.* New York: John Wiley, 1949.

Hunter, Floyd. *Community Power Structure.* Chapel Hill: University of North Carolina Press, 1953.

Hyman, Herbert. "Interviewing as a Scientific Procedure," *in* Daniel

Lerner and Harold Lasswell, eds., *The Policy Sciences*. Stanford: Stanford University Press, 1951.

International City Managers' Association. *The Municipal Yearbook* (various years). Chicago: International City Managers' Association.

Janowitz, Morris, and Dwaine Marvick. "Competitive Pressure and Democratic Consent." in Heinz Eulau, *et al.*, eds. *Political Behavior: A Reader in Theory and Research*. Glencoe, Illinois: The Free Press, 1956.

Jones, Victor. *Metropolitan Government*. Chicago: University of Chicago Press, 1942.

Jones, Victor, *et al. Metropolitan Communities: A Bibliography*. Government Affairs Foundation. Chicago: Public Administration Service, 1957.

Katz, Daniel. "Field Studies," *in* Leon Festinger and Katz, eds., *Research Methods in the Behavioral Sciences*. New York: The Dryden Press, 1953.

Kentucky University. Bureau of Community Service. *Preparing a Community Profile: The Methodology of Social Reconnaissance*. (Kentucky Community Series No. 7). Lexington: University of Kentucky, Bureau of Community Service, May, 1952.

Key, V. O., Jr. *American State Politics: An Introduction*. New York: Alfred A. Knopf, 1956.

————. *Politics, Parties and Pressure Groups*. 2d ed., rev. New York: Thomas Y. Crowell Company, 1948.

————. *Southern Politics in State and Nation*. New York: Alfred A. Knopf, 1950.

Lane, Robert E. *Political Life*. Glencoe, Illinois: The Free Press, 1959.

Lazarsfeld, Paul F., *et al. The People's Choice*. 2d ed. New York: Columbia University Press, 1948.

Lee, Eugene C. "The Politics of Nonpartisan Elections in California Cities." Unpublished doctoral dissertation. Berkeley: University of California, 1957.

Lee, Robert G. "The Berkeley Municipal Election of 1947." Unpublished master's thesis. Berkeley: University of California, 1948.

Lipset, Seymour Martin. "Political Sociology," *in* Robert K. Merton, ed., *Sociology Today*. New York: Basic Books, 1959.

Lipset, Seymour Martin, *et al.*, "The Psychology of Voting: An Analysis of Political Behavior," *in* Gardner Lindzey, ed., *Handbook of Social Psychology*, II. Cambridge, Mass.: Addison-Wesley, 1954.

Litchfield, Edward M. *Voting Behavior in a Metropolitan Area*. (Michigan Governmental Studies, no. 7.) Ann Arbor: University of Michigan Press, 1941.

Lubell, Samuel. *The Future of American Politics.* New York: Harper, 1952.

————. *The Revolt of the Moderates.* New York: Harper and Brothers, 1956.

Lynd, Robert S. and Helen M. Lynd. *Middletown: A Study in American Culture.* New York: Harcourt, Brace, 1929.

————. *Middletown in Transition: A Study in Cultural Conflicts.* New York: Harcourt, Brace, 1937.

Merriam, Charles E. *Chicago; A More Intimate View of Urban Politics.* New York: Macmillan, 1929.

Merriam, Charles E., and Louise Overacker. *Primary Elections.* Chicago: University of Chicago Press, 1928.

Merton, Robert K. "Patterns of Influence: A Study of Interpersonal Influences and of Communications Behavior in a Local Community," *in* Paul F. Lazarsfeld and Frank Stanton, eds., *Communication Research, 1948–1949.* New York: Harper, 1949.

Metropolitan Board of Freeholders, St. Louis-St. Louis County, Mo. *Proposed Plan of the Greater St. Louis City-County District.* St. Louis: Metropolitan Board of Freeholders, 1959.

Metropolitan St. Louis Survey. *Path of Progress for Metropolitan St. Louis.* University City, Mo.: Metropolitan St. Louis Survey, August, 1957.

Myerson, Martin, and Edward C. Banfield. *Politics, Planning and the Public Interest: The Case of Public Housing in Chicago.* Glencoe, Illinois: The Free Press, 1955.

Michigan. University. Institute of Social Research. Survey Research Center. *The Detroit Area Study.* Ann Arbor: University of Michigan, Institute for Social Research, Survey Research Center, July, 1955.

Munro, William Bennett. *Municipal Government and Administration* (vol. 1, "Government."). New York: Macmillan, 1923.

Myrdal, Gunnar. *An American Dilemma: The Negro Problem and Modern Democracy.* New York: Harper, 1944.

National Municipal League. *Getting the National Parties Out of Municipal Elections.* New York: National Municipal League, July, 1953.

————. *A Guide for Charter Commissions.* Rev. ed. New York: National Municipal League, 1952.

————. *A Guide for Charter Commissions.* 3d ed. New York: National Municipal League, 1957.

————. *Model County Charter.* New York: National Municipal League, 1956.

————. *A Municipal Program.* New York: Macmillan, 1900.

New, Jack L. *The Bloomington, Indiana Municipal Campaign of 1947*

(Research Study no. 27). Bloomington, Ind.: University of Indiana, Department of Government, Institute of Politics, October, 1948.

Odegard, Peter H., and E. Allen Helms. *American Politics.* 2d ed., rev. New York: Harper, 1947.

Olds, Edward B., and David W. Salmon. *St. Louis Voting Behavior Study.* St. Louis, Mo.: American Statistical Association, St. Louis Chapter, Metropolitan St. Louis Census Committee, 1948.

O'Rourke, Lawrence. *Voting Behavior in the Forty-Five Cities of Los Angeles County.* Los Angeles: University of California, Bureau of Governmental Research, 1953.

Patton, Clifford W. *The Battle for Municipal Reform: Mobilization and Attack, 1875–1900.* Washington, D.C.: American Council on Public Affairs, 1940.

Penniman, Howard R. *Sait's American Parties and Elections.* 5th ed., rev. New York: Appleton-Century-Crofts, 1952.

Pollock, James K. *Voting Behavior: A Case Study* (Michigan Governmental Studies, no. 3). Ann Arbor: University of Michigan Press, 1939.

Ramsey, Maurice M. "Some Aspects of Nonpartisan Government in Detroit, 1918–1940." Unpublished doctoral dissertation, University of Michigan, Ann Arbor, 1944.

Reed, Thomas H. *Municipal Government in the United States,* 2d. ed., rev. New York: Appleton Century, 1934.

Rossi, Alice S, and Peter H. "An Historical Perspective on the Functions of Local Politics." Unpublished paper presented at the 1956 meeting of the American Sociological Society.

Rossi, Peter H. "Community Decision Making," *in* Roland Young, ed., *Approaches to the Study of Politics.* Evanston: Northwestern University Press, 1958.

Schattschneider, E. E. *Party Government.* New York: Rinehart, 1942.

Schmid, Calvin. *Social Trends in Seattle.* (University of Washington Publications in the Social Sciences vol. 14) Seattle: University of Washington Press, 1944.

Schulz, Ernst B. *American City Government, Its Machinery and Process.* New York: Stackpole & Heck, Incorporated, 1949.

Scigliano, Robert G. "Democratic Political Organization in Los Angeles." Unpublished master's thesis. Los Angeles: University of California, 1952.

Shaffner, Margaret A. *See* Wisconsin.

Smuckler, Ralph H., and George M. Belknap. *Leadership and Participation in Urban Political Affairs.* East Lansing: Michigan State University, Government Research Bureau, 1956.

Stewart, Frank M. *A Half-Century of Municipal Reform. The History of the National Municipal League.* Berkeley and Los Angeles: University of California Press, 1950.

Stone, Harold A., Donald K. Price and Kathryn A. Stone. *City Manager Government in the United States.* Chicago: Public Administration Service, 1940.

Straetz, Ralph A. *PR Politics in Cincinnati.* New York: New York University Press, 1958.

Thompson, Warren S. *Growth and Changes in California's Population.* Los Angeles: The Haynes Foundation, 1955.

Truman, David B. *The Governmental Process.* New York: Alfred A. Knopf, 1951.

Tryon, Robert C. *Identification of Social Areas by Cluster Analysis* (University of California Publications in Psychology, 8:1) Berkeley: University of California Press, 1955.

Vidich, Arthur J., and Joseph Bensman. *Small Town in Mass Society.* Princeton, N. J.: Princeton University Press, 1958.

Walker, Robert A., and Floyd A. Cave. *How California is Governed.* New York: The Dryden Press, 1953.

Warner, W. Lloyd, and Paul S. Lunt. *The Social Life of a Modern Community.* New Haven, Conn.: Yale University Press, 1941.

Warner, W. Lloyd and Associates. *Democracy in Jonesville.* New York: Harper, 1949.

West, James. *See* Withers, Carl.

Wheeler, John Harvey. *Indiana Local Elections, 1947; Tendencies Toward Non-Traditional Voting.* (Research Study no. 26) Bloomington, Ind.: University of Indiana, Department of Government, The Institute of Politics, September, 1948.

Wisconsin. State Free Library. *Primary Elections; The Test of Party Affiliation;* by Margaret A. Shaffner. (Comparative Legislative Bulletin no. 13) Madison: Wisconsin State Free Library, December, 1908.

Withers, Carl. *Plainville, USA;* by James West [pseud.] New York: Columbia University Press, 1945.

Wood, Robert C. *Suburbia: Its People and Their Politics.* Boston: Houghton Mifflin, 1958.

Wylie, Laurence William. *Village in the Vaucluse.* Cambridge, Mass.: Harvard University Press, 1957.

Articles

Adrian, Charles R. "Some General Characteristics of Nonpartisan Elections," *American Political Science Review* XLVI (September, 1952), 766–776.

———. "A Study of Three Communities," *Public Administration Review*, XVIII (Summer, 1958), 208–213.

———. "A Typology for Nonpartisan Elections," *Western Political Quarterly*, XII (June, 1959), 449–458.

Agger, Robert E., and Daniel Goldrich, "Community Power Structures and Partisanship," *American Sociological Review*, XXIII (August, 1958), 383–392.

Bates, Frank G. "Nonpartisan Government," *American Political Science Review*, IX (May, 1915), 313–315.

Beard, Charles. "Politics and City Government," *National Municipal Review*, VI (March, 1917), 201–206.

Benney, Mark, and Phyllis Geiss. "Social Class and Politics in Greenwich," *British Journal of Sociology*, I (December, 1950), 310–327.

Binkerd, Robert S., *et al.*, "Discussion (on Political Parties in City Government)," *National Municipal Review*, VI (March, 1917), 217–237.

Bromage, Arthur. "Partisan Elections in Cities," *National Municipal Review*, XL (May, 1951), 250–253.

———. "Running for the City Council: A Case Study," *American Political Science Review*, XLIII (December, 1949), 1235–1241.

Commonwealth Club of California. "California's Nonpartisanship—Extend? Extinguish?" *Transactions*, XLVI (February 25, 1952), 55–72.

———. "Constitutional Amendments of 1915 and Nonpartisan Acts," *Transactions*, X (October, 1915), 423–486.

———. "Election Laws," *Transactions*, XV (January, 1921), 425–455.

———. Municipal Elections," *Transactions*, XI (August, 1916), 173–233.

———. "Nonpartisan Elections," *Transactions*, XXX (December 31, 1935), 93–124.

Cushman, Robert E. "Nonpartisan Nominations and Elections," *Annals of the American Academy of Political and Social Science*, CVI (March, 1923), 83–96.

Daland, Robert T. "Political Science and the Study of Urbanism," *American Political Science Review*, LI (June, 1957), 491–509.

de Grazia, Alfred. "The Limits of External Leadership Over a Minority Electorate," *Public Opinion Quarterly*, XX (Spring, 1956), 115–128.

Ellis, Ellen Deborah. "National Parties and Local Politics," *American Political Science Review*, XXIX (February, 1935), 60–67.

Farrelly, David, and Gerald Fox. "Capricious California: A Democratic Dilemma," *Frontier*, VI (November, 1954), 5–7.

Fjelstad, Ralph J. "How About Party Labels?" *National Municipal Review*, XL (July, 1955), 359–364.

Freeman, J. Leiper. "Local Party Systems: Theoretical Considerations and a Case Analysis," *The American Journal of Sociology*, LXIV (November, 1958), 282–289.

Holling, T. R. "Nonpartisan, Nonpolitical Municipal Government," *Annals of the American Academy of Political and Social Science*, CXCIX (September, 1938), 43–49.

Huckshorn, Robert J. "Spotlight on City Councilmen," *BGR Observer* (University of California, Los Angeles, Bureau of Governmental Research), (November, 1957).

Jones, Victor, and Herbert Kaufman. "The Mystery of Power," *Public Administration Review*, XIV (Summer, 1954), 205–212.

Key, V. O., Jr. "Partisanship and County Office: The Case of Ohio," *American Political Science Review*, XLVII (June, 1953), 525–532.

Ludwig, C. C. "No Place for Parties," *National Civic Review*, XLVIII (May, 1959), 237–240.

McKenzie, R. D. "Community Forces; A Study of the Nonpartisan Municipal Elections in Seattle," *Journal of Social Forces*, II (January, 1924), 266, 273; II (March, 1924), 415–421; II(May, 1924), 560–568.

Martin, Roscoe C. "The Municipal Electorate: A Case Study," *Southwestern Political and Social Science Quarterly*, XIV (1933), 193–237.

Merriam, Charles E. "Nominating Systems," *Annals of the American Academy of Political and Social Science*, CVI (March, 1923), 1–10.

Mitchell, Matthew C. "Non-partisan Nominations and Elections," *Public Business* (Rhode Island Public Expenditure Council), I (July, 1953), 4.

Morlan, Robert L. "City Politics: Freestyle," *National Municipal Review*, XXXVIII (November, 1949), 485–490.

Pearson, George W. "Predictions in a Non-Partisan Election," *Public Opinion Quarterly*, XII (Spring, 1948), 112–117.

Pitchell, Robert J. "The Electoral System and Voting Behavior: The Case of California's Cross-Filing," *Western Political Quarterly*, XII (June, 1959), 459–484.

Titus, Charles N. "Voting in California Cities, 1900–1925," *Southwestern Political and Social Science Quarterly*, VIII (1928), 383–399.

Williams, Oliver P. and Charles R. Adrian. "The Insulation of Local Politics Under the Nonpartisan Ballot," *American Political Science Review*, LIII (December, 1959), 1052–1063.

INDEX

Index